EARTH PSALMS

Earth Psalms

reflections on how
God speaks through
nature

FRANCINE RIVERS

WITH KARIN STOCK BUURSMA

Tyndale House Publishers, Inc.
Carol Stream, Illinois

Visit Tyndale online at www.tyndale.com.

Check out the latest about Francine Rivers at www.francinerivers.com.

TYNDALE and Tyndale's quill logo are registered trademarks of Tyndale House Publishers, Inc.

Earth Psalms: Reflections on How God Speaks through Nature

Designed by Jennifer Ghionzoli

Published in association with the literary agency of Browne & Miller Literary Associates, LLC,
410 South Michigan Avenue, Suite 460, Chicago, IL 60605.

LIBRARY OF CONGRESS CATALOGING-IN-PUBLICATION DATA

Names: Rivers, Francine, date, author.
Title: Earth Psalms : reflections on how God speaks through nature / Francine Rivers,
    with Karin Stock Buursma.
Description: Carol Stream, IL : Tyndale House Publishers, Inc., 2016.
Identifiers: LCCN 2016003192 | ISBN 9781496414854 (hc)
Subjects: LCSH: Nature—Religious aspects—Christianity. | Creation. |
    Devotional literature.
Classification: LCC BR115.N3 R58 2016 | DDC 233/.5—dc23 LC record available at
https://lccn.loc.gov/2016003192

Printed in China

22   21   20   19   18   17   16
8   7   6   5   4   3   2

Contents

SHOUT JOYFUL
PRAISES TO GOD,
ALL THE EARTH!
SING ABOUT THE GLORY
OF HIS NAME!
TELL THE WORLD
HOW GLORIOUS HE IS.

PSALM 66:1-2

Introduction

SCRIPTURES SAY, "For ever since the world was created, people have seen the earth and sky. Through everything God made, [we] can clearly see his invisible qualities—his eternal power and divine nature. So [we] have no excuse for not knowing God" (Romans 1:20). Everything God has created is a wonder to behold. If we look closely, we find lessons in our observations.

Writers of the Bible taught lessons through all aspects of the natural world, including plants and animals, reptiles and insects. King David used metaphors of sheep and pastures. Solomon wrote proverbs about sparrows and dogs, pigs and vipers, ants, hyraxes, locusts, and lizards. The prophets warned of how God could stop the rain and bring climate change. When Jesus walked the earth, He spoke about wheat and tares, the mustard seed, a pearl, seeds and soil.

God is an artist, and the earth and the universe are His canvas. From the microscopic complexities of an atom to the immense, expanding universe with nebulae, black holes, and galaxies, God shows His power and majesty, His attention to detail, and His great and unfailing love for us. Jesus said if people did not praise Him, "The stones will cry out!" (Luke 19:40, NIV).

When I was a girl, my family traveled, camped, and explored God's creation. I tried to do the same with my children. It's in my DNA,

so the idea of writing earth psalms as worship to the Lord sprang from my heart. Once I started, I couldn't help but praise Him for the diversity and beauty of His handiwork. I sought lessons and hidden messages in the myriad animals, plants, reptiles, and insects God has made. Now I have the privilege of sharing with you some of my observations.

Before now, I'd often considered writing a devotional, but I knew I wanted more than my limited view and personal insights. Tyndale graciously connected me with Karin Buursma, who has enriched my offering with hymns, quotes, reflections, and applications for connecting with God.

A painting is not the painter, but the passion of the artist's heart is revealed through his work. Karin and I hope this book will encourage

you to look at the world God created and search for the subtle messages that will expand your love for Him and your desire for a closer relationship with Him. So lean in, look more closely at the treasure trove, and seek Him. What lessons might God have embedded in the plants, animals, life cycles, and characteristics of His immense, complex, and marvelous creation? From the depths of the sea to the far reaches of space are countless blessings the Lord offers you. Ask the Holy Spirit to open your eyes, ears, and heart to receive what God has for you.

Enjoy!

Francine Rivers

1

Faithfulness Day & Night

The faithful love of the LORD never ends!
His mercies never cease.
Great is his faithfulness;
his mercies begin afresh each morning.

LAMENTATIONS 3:22-23

RICK AND I GET UP EARLY, and we're often treated to a sunrise casting its glow along the horizon. Early evening brings the sunset. Each winter, winds strip our oak of its broad leaves, so we can see the full blaze of glory from our deck.

Colors, so many colors. Sunrise often brings pinks, lavenders, and pale yellows that give way to pale blue above a sea of white cotton clouds. By five o'clock, the sun is going down. One night, the sky was molten hot red with streaks of fiery orange and gold. Another night, the clouds turned lavender and pink, then purple. When the sun disappeared, the sky turned indigo, then black with diamond dust tossed onto heavenly canvas.

Sunrise, sunset. Both amaze us. Each day is different, unique, rich

Satisfy us each morning with your unfailing love. PSALM 90:14

in variant hues, with swirls of gauzy cloud designs that change shape and color by the minute—all painted by the Artist as we watch in awe.

I have come to see these times of incredible beauty as God's daily greetings, a reminder that He loves us and is ever present. We are never alone. We can speak with Him anytime, day or night. Sunrise is God's "Good morning." I can look forward to the day, knowing He will guide and protect me. As Scripture tells us, "His mercies begin afresh each morning." What a wonderful promise! Yesterday's mistakes don't carry over. Today is a new beginning, and God can open my eyes to new friends, possibilities, opportunities. And then, in the

evening as the sun goes down in all its glory, God's "Good night" reassures me that I am in His hand and on His heart, and He watches over me as I sleep. Morning, evening, or in the darkest stretches of the night, He is never off duty.

> *Through many dangers, toils, and snares,*
> *I have already come;*
> *'Tis grace hath brought me safe thus far,*
> *And grace will lead me home.*

"AMAZING GRACE"

REFLECT

What does it mean that God's mercies are new, or fresh, every day? How can remembering God's faithful presence and protection give you peace as you go about your daily activities?

APPLY

This week, make an effort to view at least one sunrise and one sunset, observing the incredible beauty of our Creator. Choose one Scripture passage to read every morning and another every evening (perhaps Lamentations 3:22-23 in the morning and Psalm 121 at night). Let these truths about God's presence, mercy, and loving protection fill your mind and influence your thoughts through the day and the night.

CONNECT WITH GOD

Lord God, I am grateful for Your amazing sunrises and sunsets, which remind me of Your love and Your presence. Thank You that Your mercies begin afresh each day. Your forgiveness allows me to begin every morning anew, ready to see what You have for me. In the evening, when I lie down to sleep, may I rest in the knowledge that You have been with me all day and will continue to watch over me.

*Satisfy us each morning with your unfailing love,
so we may sing for joy to the end of our lives.*

PSALM 90:14

2

Prayer Leads to Peace

Don't worry about anything; instead, pray about everything. Tell God what you need, and thank him for all he has done. Then you will experience God's peace, which exceeds anything we can understand. His peace will guard your hearts and minds as you live in Christ Jesus.

PHILIPPIANS 4:6-7

IN THE WORDS OF WINSTON CHURCHILL, "Never give in. Never give in. Never, never, never, never." That must be the rallying call of the woodpeckers in our neighborhood, some of whom have decided the vent holes beneath our eaves are the perfect location for a new house. We've had one pesky fellow trying to widen the access to our attic. He managed to get through the wire mesh and pull out some insulation.

We wouldn't have known he was at work if he hadn't decided to put his machine-gun beak into our bedroom wall. I leapt off the Exercycle, ran to the wall, and pounded—with both fists. Silence. For one whole minute. I had no sooner returned to cycling than he was back at work. This time I ran out of the room, down the stairs, and out through the back door. He fluttered calmly away and took a break

5

on the oak down the hill. I know he was smirking; I could feel it. I went back inside. By the time I reached the bedroom, he was back at the wall, probably laughing.

Such persistence!

He reminds me of the worries that can come *rat-a-tatting* at my mind, usually late at night. The doubts and fears flutter in, and I try to *rat-a-tat* some kind of solution. Then I remember: God is God, and I'm not. Which means I have a decision to make: keep *rat-a-tatting*, or let go and let God work.

We called Stan, our contractor, and he sent out Alan to cover the woodpecker's holes with metal vents. When we find ourselves drilling our own holes through constant worry, we can cover those vulnerable places with prayer, which redirects our thought processes and keeps us focused on Jesus. And in Philippians 4, God promises that when we release our worries and turn instead to prayer, He will give us His peace—peace that's beyond anything we can understand. His peace will guard our hearts and minds from the anxieties that can be as persistent as a woodpecker.

Not to be discouraged, the woodpecker has started drilling his way into the telephone pole across the street. It's a good reminder to be diligent in prayer and not let worries flutter back and nest in my head.

"Worry is like a rocking chair: it gives you something to do, but it gets you nowhere."

ERMA BOMBECK

The Lord blesses them with peace

PSALM 29:11

Woodpeckers can peck up
to twenty times per second.

✾ REFLECT

What worries are keeping you from resting in God's peace? Spend a few minutes outside (or, if it's too wet or cold, look out a window). Look for evidence of God's presence and His loving care in nature, and remember that it extends to you, too.

✾ APPLY

This week, reread Philippians 4:6-7. When you're anxious, choose to turn away from worry and toward prayer, away from anxiety and toward God's peace.

✾ CONNECT WITH GOD

Lord, it's so easy to fall into worry. When my fears are reverberating in my mind, help me to stop trying to fix everything myself. Teach me to turn to You in prayer, trust You to be in charge, and let Your peace reign over me.

The LORD gives his people strength.
The LORD blesses them with peace.

PSALM 29:11

3

Variety in Creation

Then God said, "Let the land sprout with vegetation—every sort of seed-bearing plant, and trees that grow seed-bearing fruit. These seeds will then produce the kinds of plants and trees from which they came." And that is what happened. The land produced vegetation—all sorts of seed-bearing plants, and trees with seed-bearing fruit. Their seeds produced plants and trees of the same kind. And God saw that it was good. GENESIS 1:11-12

I LOVE WALKING THROUGH the produce section of our local grocery store and looking at all the apples—Golden Delicious, Red Delicious, Granny Smith, Gala, Braeburn, Fuji—all different colors and all beautiful. Did you know there are 7,500 kinds of apples in the world?

Apples are very interesting.

Every seed in an apple contains genetic instructions for a completely new and different apple tree. Though it seems counterintuitive, if you plant seeds from a Honeycrisp apple, the resulting tree will not produce Honeycrisp apples. The fruit could be large or small, tart or sweet, crisp or soft. The only way to reproduce one particular variety is to graft its branch onto another tree. This extreme variability is called heterozygosity, and this aspect of apples gives these trees

Romans first brought apple trees to England. Centuries later, colonists brought them to the United States. John Chapman, better known as Johnny Appleseed, is credited with spreading apple trees westward in the US.

the ability to make their home everywhere—from California to New Zealand or Kazakhstan. Every human being is unique, because we are heterozygous too.

Not only do apples smell and taste good, they are one of the many miracles of God's creation. Every single apple tree grown from a seed produces apples different in color, smell, and taste from those on any other tree. Over time, people have picked a few favorites out of God's vast crop and grafted the trees to reproduce them. Now we know what we're getting. No surprises.

That's not God's way. He loves variety in apples and in people. In Psalm 104, the psalmist exclaims, "O Lord, what a variety of things you have made!" (v. 24). The Creation account in Genesis 1 details the array of plants and creatures God made—"all sorts" of vegetation and animals, not to mention birds of the air and creatures of the sea. He could have created a much simpler natural world, but instead He made one that overflows with color, variety, and original design. And He has created humans with the same variety as well. While our culture might tell us that we have to look a certain way to be attractive, act a certain way to be well-liked, or own certain things to be successful, that boring sameness doesn't reflect God's ideal. We can revel in being part of His wonderfully varied creation.

"Whenever I am afield or outdoors, there steals over me the acute consciousness that I am confronted on every hand by the superb workmanship of my Father. It is as if every tree, rock, river, flower, mountain, bird, or blade of grass had stamped upon it the indelible label, 'Made by God.'"

PHILLIP KELLER

✻ REFLECT

In what ways do you think our culture encourages sameness? Why? How does variety in appearance, attitudes, talents, and personality reflect God's character?

✻ APPLY

This week, observe the differences in the people around you. Do you find it difficult to appreciate any of their characteristics—or any of your own? Ask God to help you value the amazing variety of His creation.

✻ CONNECT WITH GOD

Lord, at times I feel pressure to fit in with those around me. It can seem like there's only one right way to look or act. I'm so grateful that You created the world with remarkable variety—far beyond what was functional or needed, but solely for Your own pleasure and ours! Help me to value that variety in myself and others, marveling in the richness of Your creativity.

O LORD, what a variety of things you have made!
In wisdom you have made them all.
The earth is full of your creatures.
Here is the ocean, vast and wide,
teeming with life of every kind,
both large and small.

PSALM 104:24-25

4

Protective Father

The LORD your God is going ahead of you. He will fight for you, just as you saw him do in Egypt. And you saw how the LORD your God cared for you all along the way as you traveled through the wilderness, just as a father cares for his child. Now he has brought you to this place.

DEUTERONOMY 1:30-31

SOME YEARS AGO, while working at our warehouse, Rick called me on the intercom and said a mother quail was out back with her chicks. I came running, and we watched from the delivery doorway as the quail pecked for seeds and bugs among the grass behind our building. The chicks scurried around their mother like little puffs of tan cotton, unaware of us—or of danger lurking close by.

We spotted a cat crouched and sneaking toward them. Rick was about to grab an airplane gear to heave at the predator when we both heard a high-pitched chirrup from somewhere above us. The mother quail immediately spread her wings, the chicks fled beneath, and she flattened to the ground—motionless, protecting her babies with her body, and perfectly camouflaged in the grass. We stared, amazed. Then, out of nowhere, the father quail appeared. He had

Hide me in the shadow of your wings.

PSALM 17:8

been perched on the edge of the roof next door, watching and ready to signal any danger. Down he came, right at that cat. Bam! Startled, the cat jumped back. Again the male defended his family, and the frightened cat took off.

We had just witnessed a living example of what God our Father is like. Like the father quail, He watches from a high place and sees everything going on around us. He warns us when danger approaches and knows how to fight the battle to protect us from the evil one, just as He did for the Israelites entering the Promised Land. God is also our shelter, like the mother quail spreading her wings over her chicks. We can run to Him, knowing that we are safe in His presence.

God loves us with an everlasting love, and He is worthy of our complete trust. So when we hear Him warning us of danger, we need to act quickly in obedience. As Psalm 17:8 says, He will hide us in the shelter of His wings. We can rest there without fear, knowing that He is in control.

> *Under His wings I am safely abiding;*
> *Though the night deepens and tempests are wild,*
> *Still I can trust Him—I know He will keep me;*
> *He has redeemed me and I am His child.*

"UNDER HIS WINGS I AM SAFELY ABIDING"

REFLECT

How have you seen God protect you or others in the past? What dangers might He be warning you about? How can you turn to Him when trouble comes?

Quails typically make their n[...]
the ground. Their colori[...]
camouflages them in th[...]

✿ APPLY

This week, when you face a challenging situation, remember that you live in God's protection. Let your first reaction be to run to Him for security.

✿ CONNECT WITH GOD

Lord God, thank You for watching over me, for warning me when danger is near, and for protecting me. Help me never to forget how much You care for me. I trust You, Lord. I want to run to You when trouble comes.

Show me your unfailing love in wonderful ways.
By your mighty power you rescue
those who seek refuge from their enemies.
Guard me as you would guard your own eyes.
Hide me in the shadow of your wings.

PSALM 17:7-8

5

Spreading the Good News

Go and make disciples of all the nations, baptizing them in the name of
the Father and the Son and the Holy Spirit. Teach these new disciples
to obey all the commands I have given you.

MATTHEW 28:19-20

W HEN I WAS A CHILD, I loved to pick fuzzy, fluffy
dandelions. I'd blow the seeds and watch them drift away
on the breeze. Then I'd run to pick another flower. We lived in the
country, and it didn't matter if a gazillion dandelion seeds were scattered hither and yon. But in a neighborhood with pristine lawns,
blowing dandelion seeds might get you in trouble with the friends
next door who spent hours digging up weeds. The truth is, dandelions
are designed to spread. A windy day can scatter plenty of seeds even
without a little girl's help.

Another plant that spreads easily is the tumbleweed. It begins with a
small seed taking root in dry ground, and it grows from the nutrients
and moisture available. Then, drying out and dying, it breaks free from
its roots and tumbles along with the wind, casting its seeds as it rolls.

Like dandelions and tumbleweeds, our faith begins with a small seed planted by another. God provides the light and living water, allowing the seed to grow. Then we die to self and break loose from our worldly bonds, allowing the Holy Spirit to take us where God wills so that we can spread the Good News. Our words and actions are the seeds God plants, waters, and brings to new life.

If we wonder whether we're capable of spreading the gospel, Paul's words to the Corinthians can encourage us. The believers in Corinth had been arguing about which disciple they followed—Paul, Peter, or another preacher named Apollos. Paul let them know that ultimately, it didn't matter which disciple had first shared the message or had the biggest influence. He wrote, "I planted the seed in your hearts,

A large tumbleweed plant can produce as many as 250,000 seeds. Seeds can stay dormant for many years. Then, when they land in a habitable place, they can germinate within eighteen hours.

and Apollos watered it, but it was God who made it grow. It's not important who does the planting, or who does the watering. What's important is that God makes the seed grow" (1 Corinthians 3:6-7). We are not responsible for other people's spiritual growth. We're responsible for our own faithfulness in letting ourselves be used by God, in letting the wind of the Holy Spirit move us where we need to be. We have the privilege of letting people know there is a wonderful future for those who believe in Jesus, and that heaven awaits.

Be a dandelion. Be a tumbleweed. Spread the Good News.

"The work of the church is not survival. She exists to fulfill the Great Commission."
BROTHER ANDREW

❊ REFLECT

Who has been a Paul or Apollos in your life? How did they spread seeds of faith? What lessons can you take from them as you consider how God can use you to spread His Good News?

❊ APPLY

This week, tell God that you are willing to be used by Him. Pray that you would have a sensitivity to His Spirit—that you would go where He wants you to go and say what He wants you to say. Pray for the seeds of the gospel to be spread.

❊ CONNECT WITH GOD

Lord God, I want to be like a dandelion or tumbleweed, ready to be moved by the wind of Your Holy Spirit. Teach me to be responsive to Your leading, trusting in what You are asking me to do. When You give me an opportunity, may I always be willing to share with others the good news of who You are and what You have done.

*We will tell the next generation
about the glorious deeds of the LORD,
about his power and his mighty wonders.*

PSALM 78:4

6

Hard Work

Take a lesson from the ants, you lazybones.
Learn from their ways and become wise!
Though they have no prince
or governor or ruler to make them work,
they labor hard all summer,
gathering food for the winter.

PROVERBS 6:6-8

WE CONSIDER ANTS PESTS, especially in late summer when they are sending out scouts and then armies to gather food for the winter. We do our best to get rid of them with traps and poisons. Even so, they keep coming back, year after year. They are industrious, determined, and strong in the face of tremendous intolerance and persecution.

God honors them in Proverbs 30, counting them among a few animals that are "small but unusually wise" (v. 24). Why? Because ants offer good life lessons:

They work hard.

They know winter is coming.

They make preparations for the lean times ahead.

They work together.

They thrive.

They survive.

While the rest of Scripture may not be as blunt as the book of Proverbs, which refers to the listener as a "lazybones" who would do well to study the hardworking ant (see 6:6), the Bible does have more to say about work. The apostle Paul encourages the Colossians with these words: "Whatever you do, work at it with all your heart, as working for the Lord, not for human masters, since you know that you will receive an inheritance from the Lord as a reward. It is the Lord Christ you are serving" (3:23-24, NIV).

The reasons behind our work are important. Ants labor because they know their work will bring them food and shelter through the winter, and of course we do some of our work for the same reason of meeting our physical needs. But we can also labor because we know that our work—whether it's preaching a sermon, cooking a meal, teaching a classroom full of students, bagging groceries, balancing accounts, designing software, or caring for children—is for the Lord. We honor Him with our sincere effort, our good attitude, and our concern for excellence.

Rather than annihilate the anthill, I think I'll celebrate the ant this year and put a pile of brown sugar and rice in the green space just beyond our fence. Enough for a colony party.

"Work is the keystone of a perfect life. Work and trust in God."
WOODROW WILSON

An ant can lift twenty times its body weight.

REFLECT

Do you tend to think of work as something you must do to pay the bills, or do you consider it something more? How might viewing your work as something you're doing for God instead of for your human employer change your perspective?

APPLY

Think about one or two tasks that you do poorly, or with a bad attitude. This week, reread Colossians 3:23-24 and think about Paul's words when you're doing those tasks.

CONNECT WITH GOD

Lord God, thank You for giving me the opportunity to work. Teach me to imitate the industriousness of the ant—to plan for the future and to work hard even when no one is watching. May I always remember that when I work, I am really working for You. Help me to do my work to the best of my ability.

May the favor of the Lord our God rest on us;
establish the work of our hands for us—
yes, establish the work of our hands.

PSALM 90:17, NIV

food, they leave
can so... n find
o the

Community Matters

Two people are better off than one, for they can help each other succeed. If one person falls, the other can reach out and help. But someone who falls alone is in real trouble.

ECCLESIASTES 4:9-10

OUR FAMILY lives in the "Redwood Empire" of northern California, within half an hour of Armstrong Woods and two hours from the Avenue of the Giants. I've always marveled when standing inside a grove of redwood trees. Though the trees tower hundreds of feet overhead, and some of these trees are so big you can link hands with ten people and still not encircle the base, these giants have a shallow root structure. A good wind would blow one over if it were standing alone like an oak tree on a hillside. But because the redwoods grow close together, the roots are interwoven, adding strength so that when the winds come and the rains pound and soak the soil, these trees stand and continue to grow—some for more than a thousand years.

This reminds me of my church family. We come together to focus

*With God's help
we will do mighty things.*

PSALM 108:13

our hearts and minds on the Lord above, our light and our salvation. As He teaches us, we encourage one another, we embrace in joy and in sorrow, we pray for each other, and we acknowledge our need for one another. Alone we are weak and easily threatened by the winds of temptation and discouragement. But as a community of believers, we can draw strength from one another for whatever storms may come, standing firm and continuing to grow in faith.

In Ecclesiastes 4, the wise king Solomon wrote, "Two are better than one. . . . Pity anyone who falls and has no one to help them up" (NIV). If just one other person can be a source of strength, how much more can a larger community be? After all, the redwoods' roots aren't connected only to the trees on either side of them. They extend up to one hundred feet from the base of the tree in every direction—far enough to connect with scores of other redwoods. Next time

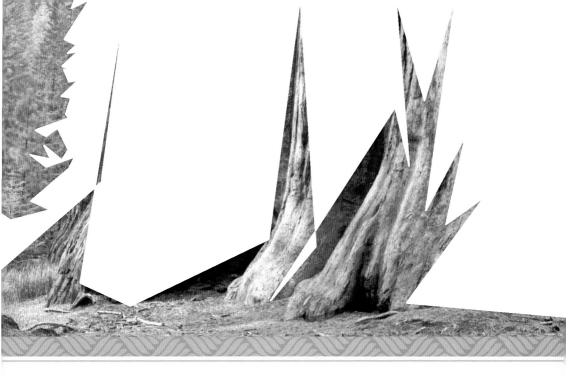

you're struggling and in need of encouragement, imagine yourself intertwined with believers all around you, held up by the combined strength of their roots. That's an image worth holding on to.

> *Blest be the tie that binds*
> *Our hearts in Christian love:*
> *The fellowship of kindred minds*
> *Is like to that above. . . .*

> *We share each other's woes,*
> *Our mutual burdens bear,*
> *And often for each other flows*
> *The sympathizing tear.*

"BLEST BE THE TIE THAT BINDS"

⚘ REFLECT

How are Christians entwined on a spiritual level even when they may not have much in common? In what ways can believers help each other stand firm in Christ?

⚘ APPLY

This week, think of one person you can lean on because he or she is part of your community in Christ. Think of someone else who is going through a hard time who might need your encouragement.

⚘ CONNECT WITH GOD

God, thank You for the community of believers of which I'm a part. I'm thankful that when I feel shaken by the challenges in my life, I can rely on the other believers who are supporting me. Help me to be a support and encouragement to them too, so that all of us will stand firm in You. Thank You that when I am rooted in You, I am connected with others who love You.

With God's help we will do mighty things. PSALM 108:13

The Colonel Armstrong tree is the oldest tree in Armstrong Woods. It's estimated to be 1,400 years old.

8

Water in the Desert

Jesus stood and said in a loud voice, "Let anyone who is thirsty come to me and drink. Whoever believes in me, as Scripture has said, rivers of living water will flow from within them." By this he meant the Spirit, whom those who believed in him were later to receive.

JOHN 7:37-39, NIV

ONE CREATURE of southwestern Africa is the *Stenocara* beetle—a little black bug with a grooved, bumpy back. It lives in the Namib Desert, one of the hottest places on Earth, where sand temperatures can reach 140 degrees Fahrenheit. Each day, this small creature climbs a sand dune before dawn and waits for the fog to announce the approaching sunrise. As it waits, tiny droplets of water form on its water-repellent casing. Once the day begins, the beetle bows its head to the ground so that the water can trickle down the waxy grooves of its back and into its mouth. And thus, even in the midst of the inhospitable desert, it receives enough water to sustain it through the day.

Our lives in this world can seem as barren as the hot desert of Namibia, but God continues to sustain us through the living water of His presence. In John 7, Jesus Himself promised that whoever was thirsty could come to Him and drink—and would find living water that would never run dry.

Jesus invites us to come to Him and be refreshed. But all too often we don't recognize our thirst for what it is. We try to fix our dissatisfaction with busyness, or material things, or friendships, or status—and we remain dissatisfied. That's as pointless as a *Stenocara* beetle who tips its head backward and lets the water droplets trickle down its back into the sand. Let's not waste the precious gift of Himself God gives us.

May we recognize our thirst for God and quench it with Him, never trying to satisfy ourselves with lesser things. May we bow in reverence to Him and receive the living water He gives us, drinking deeply and being replenished and refreshed by His promises. When life becomes

dry and barren, spend time with the Lord, who loves you and will quench your thirst.

> *I heard the voice of Jesus say,*
> *"Behold, I freely give*
> *The living water; thirsty one,*
> *Stoop down and drink and live."*
> *I came to Jesus, and I drank*
> *Of that life-giving stream;*
> *My thirst was quenched, my soul revived,*
> *And now I live in Him.*
>
> "I HEARD THE VOICE OF JESUS SAY"

31

REFLECT

When do you feel most thirsty for God? In what ways do you try to satisfy that thirst?

APPLY

Come up with a reminder—whether it's a physical note or an alarm on your computer or phone—to turn to God when you sense the dissatisfaction that is really thirst for Him.

CONNECT WITH GOD

Lord Jesus, You have offered Your very self to us, and You promise that those who are thirsty may come to You and be satisfied. Forgive me for the times when I have turned to something else—something less—in a vain attempt to make myself feel better. Teach me to turn to You and be refreshed by You, the Living Water.

As the deer pants for streams of water,
so my soul pants for you, my God.

PSALM 42:1, NIV

9

A Light for Our Path

*Your word is a lamp to guide my feet
and a light for my path.*

PSALM 119:105

M Y HOMETOWN, Pleasanton, California, used to have a lot of fog. Not a light-misting fog that stretches over the valley like a cloud lake, but a pea soup-thick fog that spreads over roads and makes driving dangerous. The seven-mile stretch home from the movie theater in the neighboring town could feel like a hundred miles. Bright lights only made the fog blind us, and low beams didn't shine past the front of the car. So we crept along, car door open, following the white lines down the middle of the road. We didn't want to end up driving over the cliff into the Kaiser gravel pits.

Angels must have been watching over us.

Angels watched over Rick, too, when the Marine Corps deployed him briefly to Yuma, Arizona, and he would hitch a ride 250 miles home to our little Santa Ana studio apartment once a week. He could

The LORD says, *"I will guide you along the best pathway for your life. I will advise you and watch over you."*

PSALM 32:8

only stay for a few hours before he and his friend had to head back to base in time for roll call. Fog lies low on those long desert roads. His friend would pull up behind a truck, close enough to see the taillights, and then stay there, foot to the floor, matching the truck driver's speed. Imagine going sixty miles an hour or more through fog, a couple of feet behind a semi.

Sometimes walking with the Lord can feel like walking in fog. We have to keep an eye on the Scriptures with every step we take so we don't get lost or sidetracked down some dark road, ending up at the edge of a cliff with a pit below. God has promised that His Word will guide us and light our way; it will be "a lamp to guide [our] feet and a light for [our] path" (Psalm 119:105). It may not function like high-wattage high beams that help us see yards ahead. In fact, His Word may be more like a candle, giving off a gentle light that illuminates only our next step. But we can trust that when His Word is guiding us, we won't take a wrong turn.

"Faith isn't the ability to believe long and far into the misty future. It's simply taking God at His Word and taking the next step."

JONI EARECKSON TADA

REFLECT

In what areas do you need God's direction? What difference does it make to trust that God has not left you in the dark—that He is directing you? How can His Word guide you?

APPLY

This week, make a commitment to turn to God's Word when you don't know what to do. Meditate on a passage of Scripture and ask God for His direction. If you're having trouble sensing His guidance, consider talking to someone who is strong in faith. He or she may be able to give you insight into what Scripture might have to say about your dilemma.

CONNECT WITH GOD

Heavenly Father, thank You for giving us Your Word, which illuminates our path. You have not left us to wander in the dark alone, but You have given us the guidance of Scripture. Help me to use it wisely and to trust Your direction.

> *For you are my hiding place;*
> *you protect me from trouble.*
> *You surround me with songs of victory.*
> *The LORD says, "I will guide you along the best*
> *pathway for your life.*
> *I will advise you and watch over you."*

PSALM 32:7-8

10

Call to Confession

*Those who trust in the L*O*R*D *will find new strength.*
They will soar high on wings like eagles.
They will run and not grow weary.
They will walk and not faint.

ISAIAH 40:31

A FRIEND CALLED FROM HAWAII and told me about an injured seagull she saw on the beach. The poor bird couldn't walk at all but flutter-hopped in its quest for food. On closer examination, my friend saw that fishing line entangled the bird's legs, hobbling it. She approached slowly, extending her hand in the hope she could remove the line and do something about the bird's wounds. Frightened, the gull flew off, legs still hobbled and infected.

Sometimes we are like that poor seagull. We become entangled in bad habits or addictions, in destructive relationships or all manner of fears. We peck away at our daily tasks, trying to forget the pain. All the while the infection of sin is growing and going deeper until it threatens to destroy us.

The seagull flew away from my friend, who wanted to untangle the fishing line and wash the wounds. We too often turn away from those who want to help us—and even from God, who is the only One who really can get rid of our sin. Sometimes we turn away out of fear, other times out of shame. More often, we turn our backs because of our pride. We don't want others to see us at our ugly worst, so we limp along, pretending we're just fine.

The pain of removing what holds us captive can be frightening. Yet if we lay aside all those things that encumber our walk with God, if we strip off the sin that slows us down, as Hebrews 12:1 says, then we find the freedom and healing that come from being reconciled to God. We no longer have to hobble about in isolation, like the injured seagull,

I confessed all my sins to you and stopped trying to hide my guilt.

PSALM 32:5

but we can live in communion with God the way we were created to. When we trust fully in God to help us and refuse to let our pride turn us away from His forgiveness, then He will renew our strength, giving us joy and energy for the tasks ahead. We will run and not grow weary; we will soar high on wings like eagles.

"To confess your sins to God is not to tell God anything God doesn't already know. Until you confess them, however, they are the abyss between you. When you confess them, they become the Golden Gate Bridge."

FREDERICK BUECHNER

✠ REFLECT

How do you react when you're struggling and someone tries to help you? When you're tangled up in sin, how do you respond to God? Why do you think we often turn away from Him? How do we benefit by letting God and others help us?

✠ APPLY

Take a moment to think about what sins, bad habits, or poor choices might be entangling you and keeping you from living with freedom. What could you do this week to throw those off?

✠ CONNECT WITH GOD

Lord Jesus, so often I let myself become constrained by sin. It trips me up, distracts me, and keeps me from living well. May I never turn away from You when I'm stuck in sin; instead, may I turn to You in humility and trust You to save me. Thank You for reaching out to heal me.

> *I confessed all my sins to you*
> *and stopped trying to hide my guilt.*
> *I said to myself, "I will confess my rebellion*
> *to the LORD."*
> *And you forgave me! All my guilt is gone.*

PSALM 32:5

An Opportunity for Joy

*Dear brothers and sisters, when troubles of any kind come your way,
consider it an opportunity for great joy. For you know that when your
faith is tested, your endurance has a chance to grow. So let it grow,
for when your endurance is fully developed, you will be perfect and
complete, needing nothing.*

JAMES 1:2-4

WE HAVE A LILAC BUSH in our backyard. I planted it ten years ago, and every year I hope to see it filled with clusters of sweet-scented blossoms. Every year I am lucky to find two small clusters on the very top.

My grandparents lived in Colorado and had a lilac hedge that filled with purple blossoms. Rick's relatives in Sweden had gorgeous lilac bushes with a profusion of clusters. Why is my lilac bush such a bust?

I live in California. The weather is nice all year round. The sky is blue and the sun shines through my window even in the dead of winter. The appearance of snow in Sonoma County is so rare it makes us ooh and aah.

Lilacs need *cold* weather. Winter snow and ice bring an abundance of spring color and scent.

Hard times often bring out the best in people, too. Some of the most striking stories of rock-solid faith in God come from enduring serious illness, job loss, personal struggles, or devastating tragedy. The worst circumstances brought about the most growth—so much so that often these believers can look back on their hardest moments and remember a strong sense of God's presence. That's because when we're faced with the unthinkable, when we're in the valley, we realize how much we need God. We grab on to Him out of desperation, and when we realize He's really there, our faith begins to grow.

James wrote these surprising words: "When troubles of any kind come your way, consider it an opportunity for great joy." Why joy? Because troubles test our faith, which builds endurance. And endurance helps us blossom into the people God created us to be.

Faith blossoms. Courage inspires.

"Remember the goodness of God in the frost of adversity."

C. H. SPURGEON

REFLECT

How have you seen God strengthen someone's faith through their difficult circumstances? When you look back at tough situations in your past, how do you think they have changed you? How would you be different if you hadn't experienced those challenges?

APPLY

What problems are you facing this week? Take a minute to consider how these challenges might be strengthening your faith. Have you

"To learn strong faith is to endure great trials.
I have learned my faith by standing
firm amid severe testings."

GEORGE MUELLER

There are over one thousand varieties of lilac bushes.
The blooms last for a couple weeks in the spring.

sensed God's presence more strongly? Do you feel God giving you the ability to endure? Thank Him for the growth you see, and commit to viewing these problems as an opportunity for more growth.

✻ CONNECT WITH GOD

Lord God, it goes against my human nature to view problems as an opportunity for joy and growth. Yet when I look back at my life and the lives of others, I know it's true. Just as some plants bloom more beautifully in spring because they experience cold in the winter, You have made us able to grow in our faith and endurance because of what we experience. Teach me to approach trouble this way. I know it will transform me.

I will be glad and rejoice in your unfailing love,
for you have seen my troubles,
and you care about the anguish of my soul.

PSALM 31:7

lilacs are among the hardier plants, some new hybrids able to withstand winter

12

Seeking Security

You can go to bed without fear;
*   you will lie down and sleep soundly.*
You need not be afraid of sudden disaster
*   or the destruction that comes upon the wicked,*
for the LORD is your security.
*   He will keep your foot from being caught in a trap.*

PROVERBS 3:24-26

A SQUIRREL COMES by every now and then. One morning he turned up his nose at the dried corncobs I put out just for him and risked his life checking out the bird feeder, only to find thistle seed. So he jumped back to the deck and began searching for acorns. Unfortunately for him, we had fewer that year. We didn't want any acorns to sprout in the yard or attract the woodpecker who wanted to drill holes and store them in our walls. So I hired one of our grandsons to pick up acorns and paid a penny each. One sand bucket carries two hundred. He filled five and felt like a millionaire.

Squirrels have a ceaseless need to keep gathering and storing food. On a visit to Oregon Caves, a ranger told us about the tons of acorns squirrels had stored in the caves—all of which had to be removed. The squirrels had turned cave rooms into warehouses, leaving little room

God is our
refuge and strength.

PSALM 46:1

for exploration. That number of acorns was far beyond what the squirrels could possibly need. But no matter how much they gathered, it never seemed to be enough.

How many of us are that way, incessantly storing for a rainy day? It's not nuts to prepare for the future, but if we think security comes from what we have in the bank, the cupboards, the closet, or the investment portfolio, we'll end up worse than disappointed. Our security is in the living God. He is our refuge and our strength, as Psalm 46 says, so we don't need to be afraid—even when our circumstances look dire. We can even state boldly, with the psalmist, "Let the oceans roar and foam. Let the mountains tremble as the waters surge!" (46:3). No trouble on earth—loss of a job, outbreak of war, illness in the family, persecution—can change the fact that the Lord reigns over all creation. He is sovereign.

Life may not work out exactly the way we think it should, and we may have to face the fact that we are not in control. But the even better truth is that God is. When the hard times come, remember that God made you, He loves you, He has a plan for your life, and He is preparing a future beyond your wildest expectations.

Fear not, I am with thee; O be not dismayed,
For I am thy God, and will still give thee aid;
I'll strengthen thee, help thee, and cause thee to stand,
Upheld by My righteous, omnipotent hand.

"HOW FIRM A FOUNDATION"

❈ REFLECT

Where do you find your security? In your abilities? Your savings? Your plans? Your job? What could be the benefits of fully trusting in God instead of relying on yourself?

❈ APPLY

What's one area of your life where you are still trying to maintain control? Tell a friend about your struggle. He or she probably has struggles too. Share with one another how you each can release your cares to God and trust in His sovereignty.

❈ CONNECT WITH GOD

Lord God, You are my rock and my refuge. Why do I need to be afraid for the future? It is all in Your hands. Help me to trust You and to believe that You will do what is best. You alone are my security.

God is our refuge and strength,
always ready to help in times of trouble.
So we will not fear when earthquakes come
and the mountains crumble into the sea.

PSALM 46:1-2

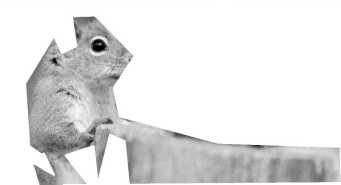

13

Prayers like Incense

When [the Lamb] took the scroll, the four living beings and the
twenty-four elders fell down before the Lamb. Each one had a harp,
and they held gold bowls filled with incense, which are the prayers
of God's people.

REVELATION 5:8

ONE SUNDAY IN JUNE, after church services, I went by
Enchanting Sweet Peas in Sebastopol. It was tucked into a
small lot next to Taco Bell—so hidden that even though I lived in
Sebastopol, I didn't know it existed until a friend told me about it.
The small farm is open to the public only one day a year. When I
arrived, there was already a gathering of people waiting with bated
breath for the 11 a.m. opening. Many people come every year to buy
seeds for new hybrid colors of sweet peas.

When the gates opened, we all swarmed in like a cloud of bees
eager to drink in the blossoms. While most lined up for seed order
forms, I just buzzed from row to row, my nose tucked as close as
possible to the sweet scent coming from pink, red, purple, white,
lavender, coral, and multicolored blossoms, row after row of heady

delight. I kept thinking about how much Mom Edith, my mother-in-law, would have enjoyed this place. Sweet peas were her favorite flower. I've been told Dad Bill looked everywhere to find her a bouquet for their December 31 wedding but failed because sweet peas are a summer flower.

The sweet scent also reminded me of how the Bible makes a connection between our prayers and sweet incense. We may not use incense much in our churches today, but it was a vital part of worship in Old Testament times, first in the Tabernacle and then in the Temple. The incense altar was to be placed just outside the curtain to the Holy of Holies—the sacred place where the Ark of the Covenant was kept. The high priest, Aaron, was to offer incense on the altar twice a day, and the Lord promised to meet with him there (see Exodus 30:6). Burning incense released a sweet aroma that was seen as an offering to God.

Our prayers are an act of worship because when we pray, we are acknowledging that God is there, that He is Lord, and that we need Him. God breathes in our prayers and smiles, answering in His time, in His way, and for our best.

Let's offer Him prayers of thanksgiving for the many blessings He has given us—including the beauty and sweet scent of summer sweet peas.

✤ REFLECT

What role does prayer play in your life? What does it mean to you that God values your prayers?

"Prayer is the link that connects us with God."

A. B. SIMPSON

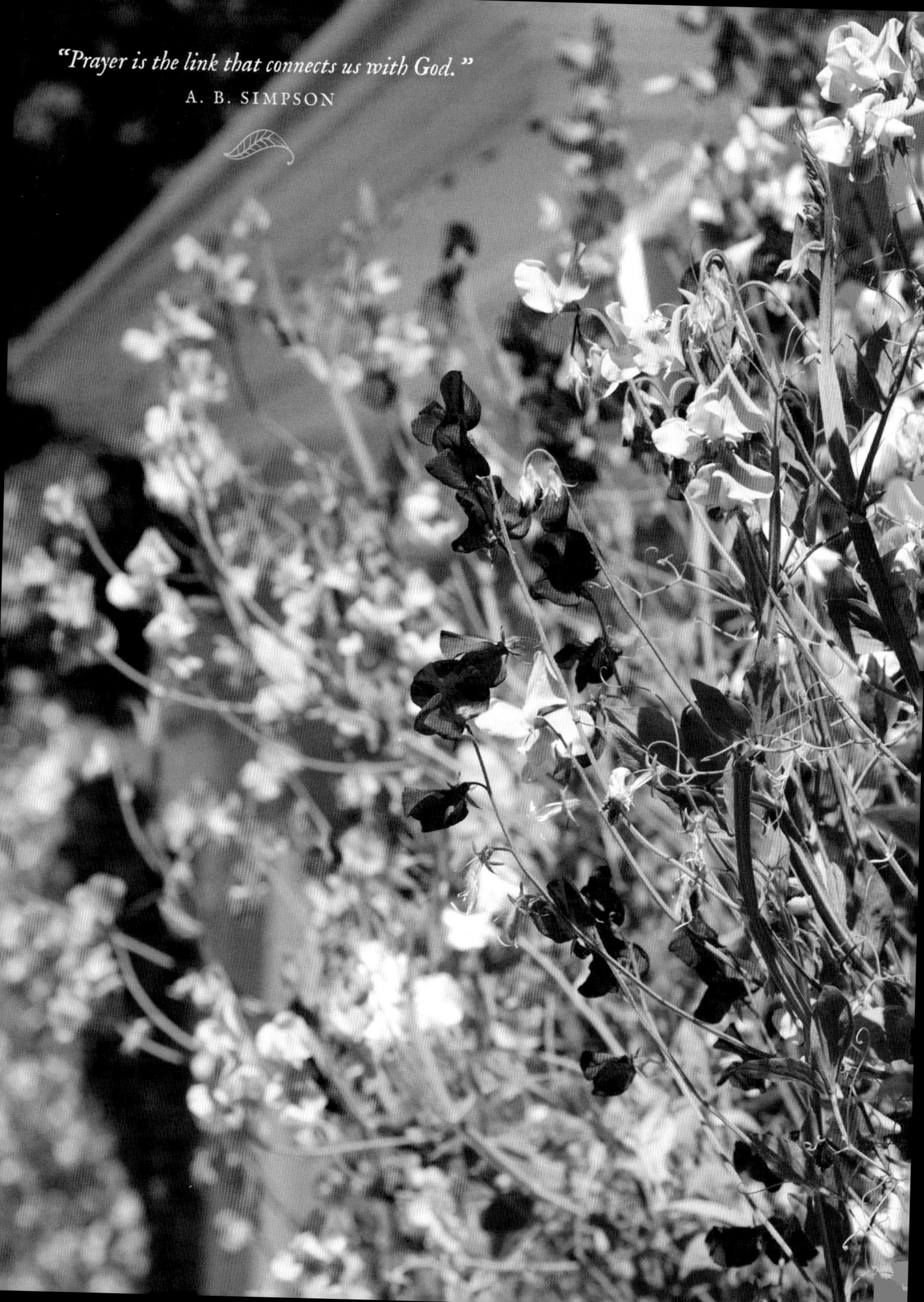

APPLY

Take some extra time for prayer this week. Consider how you might make your prayer time more worshipful. You might incorporate psalms or hymns, begin with a time of praise and thanksgiving, or reflect on God's attributes. Remember that your prayers are an act of worship, and God delights in them.

CONNECT WITH GOD

Heavenly Father, I am amazed that You value our prayers. Help me to remember that prayer is an act of worship. May I pray not only when I need something, but in times of gratitude and praise as well. You are wise, compassionate, powerful, and just—and You care about my life. I praise You! Thank You for listening to my prayers.

O LORD, I am calling to you. Please hurry!
Listen when I cry to you for help!
Accept my prayer as incense offered to you,
and my upraised hands as an evening offering.

PSALM 141:1-2

14

Learning Generosity

Remember this: Whoever sows sparingly will also reap sparingly,
and whoever sows generously will also reap generously.

2 CORINTHIANS 9:6, NIV

SOME YEARS AGO, we had a *huge* German shepherd, Hercules,
who was a full 125 pounds of muscle and energy and did not like
to share his food. We fed him just outside the sliding-glass door on
a large patio step to our deck, and sometimes he would leave a little
food in his dish for later. One afternoon, a mouse showed up for din-
ner. Herk, trapped inside the house and forced to watch this rodent
munch on his kibble, went wild. The mouse happily sat in the middle
of Herk's bowl and ate. (I think it had a smirk on its tiny face.)

Next meal, Herk ate every piece of kibble and licked the bowl
clean. He wasn't about to let that mouse get so much as a nibble of
his kibble. He came back inside, pleased with himself.

The mouse returned, in search of another free meal. Finding nothing, he looked through the window at Hercules, squatted, and left his
business card in the middle of the bowl.

It wouldn't have cost Hercules anything to share with the tiny mouse. Herk had plenty of food, a roof over his head, and a family who loved him. The little mouse only needed what amounted to one piece of kibble, but Herk never learned to share. And the mouse, in his own defiant little way, made him pay.

When we have more than enough, are we willing to share with those less fortunate? Or do we hold tight to what we have, jealous of any tiny morsel someone else might receive?

In 1 Timothy 6, the apostle Paul encourages the wealthy—and let's face it, just about all of us fall into this category—to trust in God rather than in our possessions. We need to be generous and ready to use our money to do good in the world. That's the only kind of investment that really counts. The truth is, being generous changes our hearts. When we loosen our grasp on our possessions, materialism loosens its grasp on us. Let's not be like Hercules, exhausting ourselves in our vigilance to hold on to everything we own. Let's find the freedom that comes from giving.

"It is in giving that we receive."
THE PRAYER OF SAINT FRANCIS

"Not he who has much is rich, but he who gives much."
ERICH FROMM

Good will come to those who are generous and lend freely. PSALM 112:5, NIV

Sarge, another German shepherd, is the latest addition to the Rivers family

❧ REFLECT

How have you experienced generosity from someone else? How did it affect you? Why do you think it is sometimes difficult for us to share?

❧ APPLY

Ask God to show you one way you can be generous this week, whether it's with your time, money, or possessions.

❧ CONNECT WITH GOD

Heavenly Father, I don't want to be trapped by money and the things I own, always watching out to be sure that no one else gets part of my share. I want to experience the true life that comes from being generous and holding my possessions loosely. Please help me to share with others, knowing that ultimately, everything I have comes from You.

Good will come to those who are generous and lend freely, who conduct their affairs with justice.

PSALM 112:5, NIV

15

God's Thoughtful Creation

For the LORD is God,
and he created the heavens and earth
and put everything in place.
He made the world to be lived in,
not to be a place of empty chaos.

ISAIAH 45:18

SEVERAL YEARS AGO, Rick and I took an excursion to see Claude Monet's famous garden that inspired much of his artwork. Along the way through the rural countryside, we saw numerous thatched roofs, each with a row of irises blooming on the crest. A nice creative, decorative touch, we thought. Then we learned the French discovered long ago that the roots of the iris will interlock, holding the thatch firmly from the top. (How they learned that would make an interesting investigation.) But holding a roof together is not the only benefit the flowers provide. We were also told that rats hate the smell of irises—a helpful fact when your roof is made out of vegetation.

We also saw window boxes of geraniums everywhere on our trip. Ah, so picturesque! All those beautiful splashes of vibrant color. I'd never thought about when or why window boxes came into being, but

it turns out they serve a practical purpose. For centuries, people have opened their windows to allow a fresh breeze into the house (unless, of course, their window happened to overlook a street that served as an open sewer). Most towns were built along rivers that served as trade routes. Mosquitoes flourished. Back in the days before Off! and citronella candles, the French learned that geraniums repel mosquitoes. With geraniums in a window box, people could have the benefit of fresh air without the unwelcome visitors.

God has created numerous things in nature that help solve some of our daily problems. He knew what troubles we would face after the Fall. So from Creation, He built in cures and protective resources— even before those cures and resources were needed. As Isaiah 45:18 says, He created the world to be lived in, and He put everything in place. His creation is deliberate and thoughtful, and we can see His care for us wherever we look in nature.

The world is His garden, filled with provisions for us. It's up to us to discover them and use them wisely—and with thankful hearts.

---

*"There lies all about us, if only we have eyes to see,
a creation of such spectacular profusion, such spendthrift
and extravagant richness, such intricate and absurd detail,
as to make us drunk with astonished wonder."*

MICHAEL MAYNE

*All things bright and beautiful,
All creatures great and small,
And all things wise and wonderful;
The Lord God made them all.*

*He gave us eyes to see them all,
And lips that we might tell
How great is the Almighty God
Who has made all things well.*

"ALL THINGS BRIGHT AND BEAUTIFUL"

REFLECT

What does it tell us about God that at the very creation of the world, He put measures in place to protect us and help us? How might this change the way we respond to a problem we face?

A variety of geranium called the mosquito plant geranium gives off a citronella-like scent when its leaves are crushed.

APPLY

This week when you encounter a trial, remember the irises and geraniums and think about how God already has something in place to help you through whatever you are facing.

CONNECT WITH GOD

Lord God, I can't even fathom Your wisdom. Even before sin had come into the world, You knew that people would need Your help, and You built help into your creation. Thank You for caring for us so much that even this fallen world is full of examples of your grace and kindness.

The heavens are yours, and the earth is yours;
everything in the world is yours—you created it all.

PSALM 89:11

16

Lessons in Risk Taking

For God has not given us a spirit of fear and timidity,
but of power, love, and self-discipline.

2 TIMOTHY 1:7

OUR FAMILY HAS had many kinds of pets, and one of the most interesting was a turtle. He lived in an aquarium with nice rocks that he could climb. He ate live fish (which was disturbing to watch) and did not appreciate being handled. If someone picked him up, he would disappear inside his shell.

After Rick read an article warning that such turtles carry salmonella, he decided the turtle had to go. The children and I took a drive out to the coast and stopped in at a ranch reputed to welcome retired horses. We had seen a large pond with rushes and wild birds (none big enough to carry off a turtle), and we asked if we could release our turtle there. The gentleman in charge said yes.

We tearfully trekked down the hill to the pond and set the turtle on the bank. He didn't move. He had retreated so deeply into his shell, even his nose didn't stick out. We waited, hoping. We tried to reason with him: "Look at that beautiful pond. Look at all those rushes and that log out there. There's probably a girl turtle waiting for you. You can have little turtlettes."

Finally he peered out, and it was time for us to go. Still a little sad, we headed back up the trail.

Probably all of us have retreated like the turtle at times, too afraid to venture out of the safe shells we've built around ourselves. But if we don't take the risk and stick our necks out, we might miss the wonderful things God has planned for us.

The apostle Paul's words, originally written to his protégé Timothy, can encourage all of us: God has not given us a spirit of timidity. No matter how afraid we feel, the truth is that God has given us His Holy Spirit, and fear has no part of Him! Next time you feel like a turtle, playing it safe behind the walls of protection you've erected, remember that God's Spirit is in you, giving you power, love, and self-discipline.

REFLECT

In what areas of your life are you trying to protect yourself by pulling back? How might the barriers you've erected be keeping you from experiencing God's best for you?

APPLY

Choose one specific thing to do this week to "stick your neck out" and take a risk, remembering that God has not given you a spirit of fear.

"A ship in harbor is safe,
but that is not what ships are built for."

JOHN A. SHEDD

❈ CONNECT WITH GOD

Dear God, so often I feel like a turtle, retreating into my shell because it's safe. But making safety my first priority won't lead to growth. I don't want to miss the opportunities around me because I'm too afraid to take a risk. You have given me a spirit of courage. Please help me to trust You, to trust Your love for me and Your good plans for my life. Help me to move forward in courage.

I prayed to the LORD, and he answered me.
He freed me from all my fears.
Those who look to him for help will be radiant with joy;
no shadow of shame will darken their faces.

PSALM 34:4-5

17

Planting Seeds of Faith

All glory to God, who is able, through his mighty power at work within us, to accomplish infinitely more than we might ask or think.

EPHESIANS 3:20

OUR CHURCH has few parking spaces, and the fire department has graciously allowed us to use the lot next to their building. As we walk from the lot to church, we pass by a barrel filled with dirt that serves as a planter. There isn't much in it, other than a few volunteer pansies. Seeds have apparently dropped, because those delicate kitten faces smile up at us from other places along the way, including cracks in the concrete pathway.

Pansy comes from the French word *pensée*, which means "thought." In the fifteenth century, this little flower was the symbol of remembrance. With over 400 varieties, pansies are a popular annual and biennial for gardeners who once considered "heart's ease" (another name) a weed. These lovely multicolored flowers are one of my favorites, because they are hardy, require little care, and spread quickly.

Pansy seeds blow and grow wherever they land, often in unexpected places. They're able to take root even in a tiny bit of soil in a cracked sidewalk. Against all odds, they grow. I think of Christians who live in countries where the soft soil of religious freedom has been covered by the hard cement of oppression. From a human perspective, faith seems impossible in the midst of persecution or trial. Yet God plants a seed of faith, and the seed sprouts and grows. A person's life, planted where only God could bring growth, becomes beautiful, and that life is noticed—a marvel of beauty in the barrenness.

In Ephesians 3:20, the apostle Paul reminds us that God is capable of doing far more than we can even imagine or would ever dare to ask. He can change the hardest of hearts. He can make faith flourish in the worst of circumstances. He can create beauty out of ashes. Nothing is impossible for Him.

"Faith expects from God what is beyond all expectation."

ANDREW MURRAY

REFLECT

When have you seen faith growing in an unlikely place? What does this reveal about God's power and faithfulness?

APPLY

This week, visit OperationWorld.org or use another resource to learn about a country where Christian brothers and sisters face persecution. Spend time praying that God would cause faith to grow even in that challenging landscape.

Pansies are edible and have a mild wintergreen taste.

✾ CONNECT WITH GOD

Lord, I'm grateful that You can make faith grow in even the unlikeliest of places. Where we see barrenness, You see potential. Where we see hopelessness, You see possibility. I praise You for Your power and for Your compassion in causing our faith to grow. Help me to remember that nothing is too difficult for You. Please strengthen those believers throughout the world who face persecution. May Your name be magnified through their faith.

I will thank you, Lord, among all the people.
I will sing your praises among the nations.
For your unfailing love is as high as the heavens.
Your faithfulness reaches to the clouds.

PSALM 57:9-10

18

Responding with Thanks

Be thankful in all circumstances, for this is God's will for you who belong to Christ Jesus.

1 THESSALONIANS 5:18

ONE DAY, I noticed a battle going on in the skies overhead. Crows were attacking a red-tailed hawk. These weren't small birds defending a nest; they were like a gang of bullies circling their victim. The hawk didn't return the attack, though there were several times when it looked like with a swift rollover, he could have grasped one of the smaller birds and had a tasty snack. Instead, the hawk dodged and gave a flap or two of his powerful wings to gain a little more height. In ever-increasing circles the hawk soared higher and higher, until the crows gave up and flew away.

Life's problems can seem like a gang of bullies after us. People and situations "peck" at us all the time, and we can feel under attack. What do we do when we are surrounded by trouble?

We can take a lesson from the red-tailed hawk. We don't have to use up our energy engaging with problem people or worrying about our circumstances. Instead, we can use our wings of faith to take us higher and closer to God. We study God's Word. We pray. We remember the times in the past when God was there for us. And as 1 Thessalonians 5:18 tells us, we give thanks in all things, in all circumstances. That very act of gratitude changes our perspective, reminds us that all is not lost, and reassures us that God is present in our situation. When we live in thankfulness, we can remember that in all things, God works for the good of those who love Him (see Romans 8:28). He promised! Every time we face a problem, we can remember His promise and look for His hand.

We are in a spiritual battle every day of our lives while living inside these temporal bodies on this fallen earth. But we can still live with thanksgiving because of God's promises. With His help, we can soar in the midst of tribulation.

"Reflect upon your present blessings—
of which every man has many—not on your past
misfortunes, of which all men have some."

CHARLES DICKENS

REFLECT

How is gratitude tied to our perspective on our circumstances? How can living with deliberate thankfulness change our attitudes?

Crows are intelligent birds who sometimes steal food from others. They have been known to follow adult birds to discover where their nests are—and then eat the eggs.

APPLY

Take a few minutes each day this week to write down five things you're thankful for. Challenge yourself to thank God even for some hard things in your life.

CONNECT WITH GOD

Lord God, sometimes the command to be thankful in all circumstances seems impossible. Teach me how to live with gratitude. May I never forget that You are with me, and You are working in all things for my good. No matter what else happens, that's something to be thankful for.

Enter his gates with thanksgiving;
go into his courts with praise.
Give thanks to him and praise his name.
For the LORD is good.
His unfailing love continues forever,
and his faithfulness continues to each generation.

PSALM 100:4-5

19

Slow & Steady Transformation

The Lord—who is the Spirit—makes us more and more like him as we are changed into his glorious image.

2 CORINTHIANS 3:18

WHILE ON A VOYAGE through the Inside Passage of Alaska a few years ago, we cruised into Tracy Arm, a fjord near Juneau, to see the Sawyer Glaciers. We were fortunate enough to have a balcony, and we sat dressed in bathrobes with steaming cups of coffee as the ship turned around, giving us a phenomenal view. Ice is usually clear or sometimes white, but a glacier has blue within it. Over centuries, feet of snow are packed down year after year. As weight and pressure increase, the dense ice absorbs every other color of the spectrum except blue, which is what we see.

Glaciers move slowly, scraping away plants and trees, crushing boulders into gravel, reshaping mountains, creating canyons. When a glacier reaches the sea, sections break off (calve) and fall, becoming

Search me, O God, and know my heart.

PSALM 139:23

About 75 percent of the
world's freshwater is stored in glaciers.

icebergs in the cold green ocean. You don't see the glacier moving day by day, but you see the evidence of movement.

We don't always see the Holy Spirit moving within us, either, but the evidence of His presence is that our "lifescape" is changing. Our decision to accept Christ as Savior and Lord may not seem to make a difference in our lives at first, but we can trust that God is working. If we are willing, He will use every trial and tribulation from this life to transform us into the "glorious image" of His Son, Jesus. It is a process, one that begins at our conversion and doesn't end until Christ's return. Philippians 1:6 assures us of this reality: "God, who began the good work within you, will continue his work until it is finally finished on the day when Christ Jesus returns." Like the path of a glacier, the evidence will be revealed.

God made us in His image so that we can reveal His glory through our transformed lives. We can live in a way that brings change—not only within us, but in our relationships, our communities, our country, and our world. Small, unnoticed changes over time make a big difference—in nature and in a single human life.

"The same Jesus who turned water into wine can transform your home, your life, your family, and your future. He is still in the miracle-working business, and His business is the business of transformation."

ADRIAN ROGERS

REFLECT

What does it mean to be changed into God's image? Why do you think God chooses to sanctify us gradually? What changes has God made in your life in the time you've been walking with Him, and what further transformation are you hoping to see?

APPLY

If you feel discouraged because you aren't seeing transformation in your life, take a moment to look back over the past months and recall the areas where you most struggled. How are you different than you once were? Even if the struggles have not changed, perhaps the way you respond has. If you're still not sure if you have changed, ask a friend how he or she sees you being transformed into God's image.

CONNECT WITH GOD

Heavenly Father, thank You for working in my life. Even in those moments or days or months when I feel like I'm exactly the same as I used to be, help me to trust that You are faithful to complete Your work in me. I praise You because You are transforming me into Your glorious image! I want to be open to the work of Your Spirit; I want to be more like You. May I always be ready to listen and learn.

Search me, O God, and know my heart;
test me and know my anxious thoughts.
Point out anything in me that offends you,
and lead me along the path of everlasting life.

PSALM 139:23-24

20

Something Small in God's Hands

"The Kingdom of Heaven is like a mustard seed planted in a field. It is the smallest of all seeds, but it becomes the largest of garden plants; it grows into a tree, and birds come and make nests in its branches." Jesus also used this illustration: "The Kingdom of Heaven is like the yeast a woman used in making bread. Even though she put only a little yeast in three measures of flour, it permeated every part of the dough."

MATTHEW 13:31-33

WHENEVER IT RAINS, earthworms come up out of their burrows and squirm above the ground. Usually, I grimace and toss them back into the garden. Remember the old song "Worms crawl in, worms crawl out . . ."? Worms used to make me think of death and decay. Not anymore.

Much to my family's amusement, I read *The Earth Moved*, Amy Stewart's book about earthworms, and was fascinated. Did you know that earthworms alter soil composition, increasing its capacity to absorb water and bringing increased nutrients and microorganisms? Worms pass the top few inches of soil through their innards each year, returning fertile castings to the dirt.

Worms can change an environment, cleaning soil and restoring land. Some cities are building massive worm composters called "continuous flow reactors" that turn sewage into usable soil and use recycled water to create new wetlands that support endangered species like the great blue heron.

I may start composting just to observe these fascinating creatures. They love banana peels, melon rinds, coffee grounds, lettuce leaves. Think of it! Come spring, the worms will have turned table scraps into natural fertilizer to make my garden grow.

How like God to use something small to change something big.

In Matthew 13, Jesus compares the Kingdom of Heaven to two small things—a mustard seed and a bit of yeast. Even though the seed is tiny, it grows into a large tree that serves as a home for many birds. And even though there's only a little yeast in the bread dough, it makes the whole loaf rise.

From a human perspective, it doesn't make sense that something so small could have such a large effect. But in the Kingdom of God, all things are possible. Size doesn't matter to God. He doesn't need us to be big or powerful or mighty, because He is all of those things. If we want to further the Kingdom of Heaven, if we want to serve God, all we need to do is be faithful. Be willing to be used. He will do the rest.

"Always keep your eyes open for the little task, because it is the little task that is important to Jesus Christ. The future of the Kingdom of God does not depend on the enthusiasm of this or that powerful person; those great ones are necessary too, but it is equally necessary to have a great number of little people who will do a little thing in the service of Christ."

ALBERT SCHWEITZER

"I am only one, but still I am one.
I cannot do everything, but still I can do something.
And because I cannot do everything,
I will not refuse to do the something that I can do."

EDWARD EVERETT HALE

Earthworms are able to remove
E. coli and salmonella from sewage

✠ REFLECT

The Bible is full of stories of people who were weak or unimportant but did great things for God—people like David (the youngest of his brothers), Moses (who didn't speak well and asked God to choose someone else to lead the Israelites), and Mary (a young, powerless girl). Why do you think God uses seemingly insignificant people to accomplish big things? What does it show us about His character?

✠ APPLY

Do you ever feel too small or insignificant to accomplish anything for God? This week, choose one of the Bible characters mentioned above and read his or her story. (The anointing of David: 1 Samuel 16. God choosing Moses: Exodus 3. The angel appearing to Mary: Luke 1.) Think or journal about how God used that person in a mighty way. Let this encourage you as you consider your own life.

✠ CONNECT WITH GOD

Lord God, in our culture, usually the smartest, the strongest, the most attractive, and the wealthiest win. I'm grateful that in Your Kingdom, You turn that all around. I am amazed when I consider all the small things You use to accomplish great things. Thank You for the examples throughout the Bible of people who weren't that strong or smart or brave. But they were willing—and You did the rest. Help me to be willing to let You use me. I want to be a part of spreading Your Kingdom.

In your strength I can crush an army;
with my God I can scale any wall.

PSALM 18:29

21

Following the Good Shepherd

My sheep listen to my voice; I know them, and they follow me.
I give them eternal life, and they will never perish. No one can
snatch them away from me.

JOHN 10:27-28

IN SCRIPTURE, God often refers to His people as sheep—which made me wonder what attributes I share with the reputedly dumb animal.

Sheep are born with the strong instinct to follow other sheep. Put a bold or curious one out in front and the rest will trail behind. It's called "flock mentality." All is well as long as the leader isn't heading for a patch of poisonous weeds or craggy cliffs.

Sheep are gregarious. They stay in a group while grazing and are highly agitated when left alone. They're vulnerable too; when on their own, they fall prey to predators. They're easily frightened and quickly scattered.

Sheep never walk a straight line. Instead, they wander and turn, looking behind them with first one eye and then the other. They also

> *"Some Christians try to go to heaven alone, in solitude; but believers are not compared to bears, or lions, or other animals that wander alone; but those who belong to Christ are sheep in this respect, that they love to get together. Sheep go in flocks, and so do God's people."*
>
> C. H. SPURGEON

depend heavily on their acute hearing and keen sense of smell to warn them of enemies.

Do any of those traits sound familiar? People too have a flock mentality—only we call it peer pressure. If we don't pay close attention to our leaders, we'll follow them right into new ideas that pull us away from God's truth. Just like sheep, we are vulnerable when isolated, giving in more easily to temptation. We're prone to wander away from God and the church, spending less time in the Word, watching our lives unravel, and even blaming God for abandoning us when we were the ones who left. We need the accountability that comes from the

body of Christ. Only then will we remember to look for answers in the Lord alone. Finally, like sheep, we face danger, so we need to be alert. Reading Scripture will keep our spiritual eyes and ears sharp.

I am a sheep! I'm going to stay in God's fold and stick close to the Good Shepherd. Where He goes, I'm going. I'll listen for His voice and run after Him when He calls. When the enemies come (false teachers, God mockers), I will be safe in Him. No one can ever snatch me away from my Shepherd. And when the day is over, I will lay my head on His feet and smile, content and full of thanksgiving for the new dawn coming.

REFLECT

Which of the sheep characteristics do you identify with? When are you tempted to wander away from God or fall into "flock mentality"? What spiritual dangers do you face?

APPLY

Read one or more of the following passages: John 10:1-18, 25-30; Psalm 23; Ezekiel 34:11-16. Take some time to consider the idea of Jesus as our Good Shepherd, who knows our weaknesses and yet diligently cares for us. Think about how you can better recognize and follow His voice.

CONNECT WITH GOD

Lord God, I know that I am like a sheep in so many ways. I am weak, easily frightened, a follower, vulnerable, with a tendency to wander away from what is good. Thank You for being the Good Shepherd who protects and cares for His sheep. Help me to train myself to know Your voice and listen for it. May I always stay close to You, my guide and protector.

The LORD is my shepherd;
I have all that I need.
He lets me rest in green meadows;
he leads me beside peaceful streams.

PSALM 23:1-2

22

Testing the Boundaries

_When the Son of Man comes in his glory, and all the angels with him,
then he will sit upon his glorious throne. All the nations will be gathered
in his presence, and he will separate the people as a shepherd separates
the sheep from the goats. He will place the sheep at his right hand and
the goats at his left._

MATTHEW 25:31-33

W E'VE SEEN that Scripture often compares the people of
God to sheep. But some of those same Scripture passages
go on to compare people who _aren't_ following God to goats—and the
comparison isn't flattering. How are goats different from sheep?

While sheep graze primarily on grass, goats will eat anything they
can find: clothes off a line, dog food (a favorite), toys, grass, vegetables, cardboard, and even some toxic plants.

Goats are extremely curious and intelligent. They're easily trained,
but they're also known for escaping pens. They test fences and will
climb on or push through barriers.

Rather than staying together like sheep, goats spread out. They
seldom feed side by side. Goats fight, butt, make a lot of noise, have
turf wars, and play favorites with their kids or abandon them.

O, to grace how great a debtor
Daily I'm constrained to be!
Let that grace, Lord, like a fetter,
Bind my wand'ring heart to Thee.
Prone to wander, Lord, I feel it;
Prone to leave the God I love;
Here's my heart; Lord, take and seal it;
Seal it for Thy courts above.

"COME, THOU FOUNT OF EVERY BLESSING"

It's not hard to recognize human behaviors in these characteristics. We all know people who will "eat" anything, who are always looking for new ideas and new relationships. They have an off-with-the-old-and-on-to-the-new way of thinking, but some of those new ideas are poison to the soul. These "goats" may look full and rich, but they are really only harming themselves, heading toward life without God.

Testing barriers? Some people feel trapped by rules meant to protect them from harm. They rebel and push away any restraint in order to experiment with drugs, alcohol, sex, crime, or whatever appeals at the moment. Sometimes they suffer the consequences. Often they cause those around them to suffer as well.

What about fighting with each other instead of functioning as a community? I could name a few politicians who fit that description. A few church leaders as well. That kind of conflict is rooted in selfishness and a "me first" attitude that keeps people from remembering that we're created to be part of a flock.

We've already seen that sheep have more than their share of defects. But even with all their struggles—their wandering, their timidity, their tendency to follow the crowd—they have one characteristic we need to embrace wholeheartedly: they listen to their shepherd.

I'd rather be a sheep grazing in the pastures of the Lord than be a goat nibbling the chaff Satan feeds his flock. How about you?

❈ REFLECT

Why are we so prone to desiring new things, testing barriers, and fighting for our own territory? How can we combat those tendencies?

✴ APPLY

Identify one way you push the boundaries, compete with others, or continually look for new ideas. Ask God to help you respond like a sheep rather than like a goat. Reflect on the idea of following the Good Shepherd.

✴ CONNECT WITH GOD

Good Shepherd, help me to remember that You have my well-being in mind. The boundaries You set are not to frustrate me but to keep me safe. Keep me from following my own way. Teach me instead to follow You like a sheep, always listening to Your voice and knowing that's how I will find my way to You.

He led his own people like a flock of sheep,
guiding them safely through the wilderness.
He kept them safe so they were not afraid;
but the sea covered their enemies.

PSALM 78:52-53

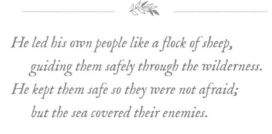

Different breeds of goats can be drastically different sizes. The two hundred breeds in the United States range in size from 20 pounds (Nigerian dwarf goat) to 250 pounds (Anglo-Nubian goat).

23

Glorious Creation

*[The angel] took me in the Spirit to a great, high mountain, and
he showed me the holy city, Jerusalem, descending out of heaven from
God. It shone with the glory of God and sparkled like a precious stone—
like jasper as clear as crystal.*

REVELATION 21:10-11

ONE OF THE PLACES I would like to visit (again) is
Holland. I've visited twice, and each time I missed the spring
tulip season with the stripes of color filling vast acres of land.

The Ottoman Turks were the first to discover wild tulips. *Tulip*
in Turkish means "turban," and these particular turbans were gorgeous. In the 1550s, an Austrian Hapsburg ambassador to the court of
Süleyman the Magnificent in Constantinople stole a few bulbs and
sent them west. The Dutch, who had limited land space, filled their
window planters with the colorful flowers. "Tulip mania" spread like
wildfire. Prices climbed until people were spending a fortune on a
single bulb. But what goes up eventually comes down (like a housing
market!), and the tulip market crashed.

The beautiful, brilliantly colored tulips we see today aren't the same as those Ambassador de Busbecq sent west. Tulips have been hybridized and have lost their original splashes ("breaks") of color. While some wild tulips still exist, the tulips of Süleyman's day can mainly be seen only in Middle Eastern paintings and ceramics.

As beautiful as today's tulips are, God's original design was far more magnificent. Such is man's inability to improve on God's work. He is the master Designer and ultimate Creator, and He specializes in breathtaking color, eye-opening variety, and awe-inspiring beauty. If that's what He created on earth, which is our temporal home, imagine what He has created in heaven, our eternal home and His. We have the promise that heaven is far more amazingly beautiful than anything we can even imagine—and hopefully the one place in the universe where we will see God's gloriously created tulips growing in His garden.

God reveals Himself to us through His creation. The beauty we see around us now is a reminder of His majesty and beauty, and it's a promise of even more majesty and beauty to come. Someday we'll not only view the fullness of His creation, but we'll be able to see Him face-to-face. That will be beautiful beyond all imagining.

❀ REFLECT

What do you think heaven will be like? Based on Scripture passages such as Revelation 21 and 22:1-6, how do you picture it? What might change in your life if you thought about heaven each day? What does God's creation tell us about God Himself and His love for us?

*"We may speak about
a place where there are
no tears, no death, no fear,
no night; but those are just
the benefits of heaven.
The beauty of heaven
is seeing God."*
MAX LUCADO

APPLY

Take a few minutes to read Revelation 21-22:6 and reflect on the promise of heaven. Thank God for His goodness to us.

CONNECT WITH GOD

Heavenly Father, I praise You because You are the master Designer! I know that the heaven You have created will be beautiful beyond my wildest imagination. I don't know how to thank You for saving me and welcoming me to this beautiful place. Help me to live each day with heaven in mind. May I remember that the greatest moment of heaven will be viewing You face-to-face.

The heavens proclaim the glory of God.
The skies display his craftsmanship.
Day after day they continue to speak;
night after night they make him known.

PSALM 19:1-2

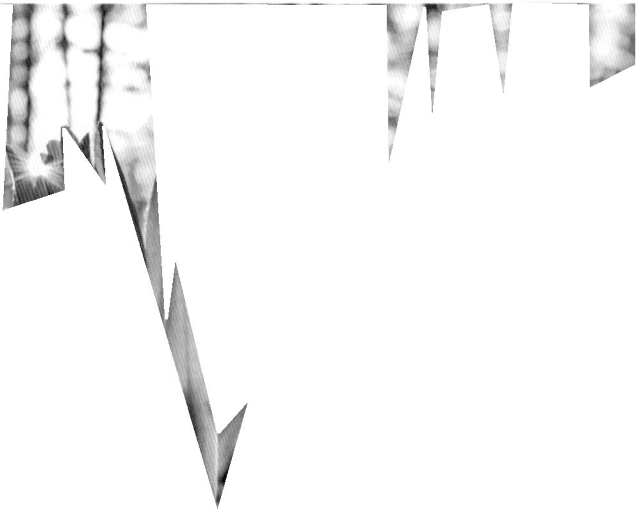

24

Godly Protection

The LORD went ahead of them. He guided them during the day with a pillar of cloud, and he provided light at night with a pillar of fire. This allowed them to travel by day or by night. And the LORD did not remove the pillar of cloud or pillar of fire from its place in front of the people.

EXODUS 13:21-22

WHILE IN SPAIN on a bus tour with Rick's sister and brother-in-law, we saw umbrella pines lining some major thoroughfares and highways. These roads were first constructed by the efficient Roman Empire, which built almost 250,000 miles of roads throughout areas that are now Europe, the Middle East, and northern Africa. Hence the old saying that all roads lead to Rome—literally true at one point in history! Apparently the pines were planted because Roman soldiers preferred patrolling their conquered territories in the shade. I'm thankful they introduced these lovely trees that offer cooler temperatures in the heat of the day.

The umbrella trees reminded me of how the Lord appeared as a cloud and led His people as they traveled through the wilderness. Psalm 105 says He "spread a cloud above them as a covering" (v. 39).

He knew they couldn't stand the heat—and I mean that in more ways than one. Sometimes seeing is believing, and seeing the Lord in the form of a cloud was a constant reminder: "I am with you. Follow Me." When the cloud rose, the Israelites broke camp and followed. When the cloud settled, they pitched their tents and rested. At nighttime, a pillar of fire lit the sky.

God's presence in the cloud played an enormous role when the Israelites were escaping from Egypt. The Israelites seemed trapped up against the Red Sea. But the cloud moved behind them, creating a barrier between them and the Egyptian army that turned to fire as night fell and was only lifted when the people had safely crossed on dry ground (see Exodus 14). God's protection was so real, so tangible, that people could almost reach out and touch it.

The Lord is our protection against the heat of living in a fallen world. He is the light when darkness comes. He is the One who knows the path through the wilderness to the Promised Land of heaven. Follow Him!

Open now the crystal fountain,
Whence the healing stream doth flow;
Let the fire and cloudy pillar
Lead me all my journey through;
Strong deliverer, strong deliverer,
Be Thou still my strength and shield,
Be Thou still my strength and shield.

"GUIDE ME, O THOU GREAT JEHOVAH"

✖ REFLECT

How did the pillars of cloud and fire give the Israelites confidence as they headed into the wilderness? How can we have confidence in God's leading today when we lack such visible evidence of His presence?

✖ APPLY

Identify one or two areas where you most need God's guidance and protection. This week, pray for His help and remember that He is leading you.

✖ CONNECT WITH GOD

Lord God, You led the Israelites in a mighty way. I can't imagine the awe they must have felt when they saw the pillar of cloud and the pillar of fire going ahead of them through the Red Sea and the wilderness. Help me to remember that You are leading me too. Even though I don't see You, You are still my protection, my light, and my guide.

The LORD spread a cloud above them as a covering
and gave them a great fire to light the darkness.

PSALM 105:39

Umbrella pine trees, or stone pines, are valued
for their seeds, which we know as pine nuts.

25

Staying Close to the Master

Care for the flock that God has entrusted to you. Watch over it willingly, not grudgingly—not for what you will get out of it, but because you are eager to serve God.

1 PETER 5:2

BOTH DOGS AND CATS have taught me lessons about faith. A dog loves unconditionally, accepting discipline and holding no resentment. A dog follows its master and likes to be right at his or her feet. Our dog Shabah was always where we were. When we went upstairs to bed, he planted himself right in our doorway. In the morning, he sat on my feet or Rick's while we did our devotions together. He was easily trained because he wanted to please us. If he needed something, he let us know through his manner and his "puppy dog look": "I have to go out." "Please . . . please . . . please throw the tennis ball." "Give me a scratch." We always responded. Shabah died, but now Sarge is much the same.

I had numerous cats when I was a child, and cats are lovely but independent. They don't need to be with the "master" at all times. In fact, cats seem to think they are the masters of their own realms. "Here, kitty, kitty," doesn't always bring them running. Sometimes cats will look at you with that "what do you want?" expression, and sometimes they'll find a nice quiet place and just plain ignore you. On the plus side, petting them is said to reduce stress. Who can resist that rumbly purring sound they make when they're being stroked? But affection has to be on their own terms. They'll come when they're called as long as you're offering food or milk. If there isn't something in it for them, they'll come when they please.

Don't get me wrong; I love both dogs and cats. But in matters of faith, I don't want to be like a cat, thinking I can call the shots and do my own thing. I want to be like a dog. I want to be at my Master's feet. I want to serve Him the way the apostle Peter describes: "willingly, not grudgingly—not for what [I] will get out of it, but because [I am] eager to serve God." When I hear God's quiet voice, I want to come running, grinning from ear to ear, ready to do whatever He asks.

✵ REFLECT

What are some ways we are catlike in our response to God? Why do we like to be our own masters? How can we change our tendencies and be willing to humbly trust God's way?

✵ APPLY

A dog learns to love his master by spending time with his master. This week, make an effort to spend extra time with God. Picture yourself sitting at His feet and enjoying His presence. Ask Him to grow your love for Him and your eagerness to serve.

"We don't follow Him in order to be loved;
we are loved, so we follow Him."

NEIL ANDERSON

CONNECT WITH GOD

Lord God, I want to be wholehearted in my devotion to You, loving You fully and unconditionally because You are my God and You care for me. Teach me to be loyal, to remain close to You, and to be eager to do Your will. May I serve You with my whole heart, not out of duty but out of pure love for who You are.

I will praise you as long as I live,
lifting up my hands to you in prayer.
You satisfy me more than the richest feast.
I will praise you with songs of joy.

PSALM 63:4-5

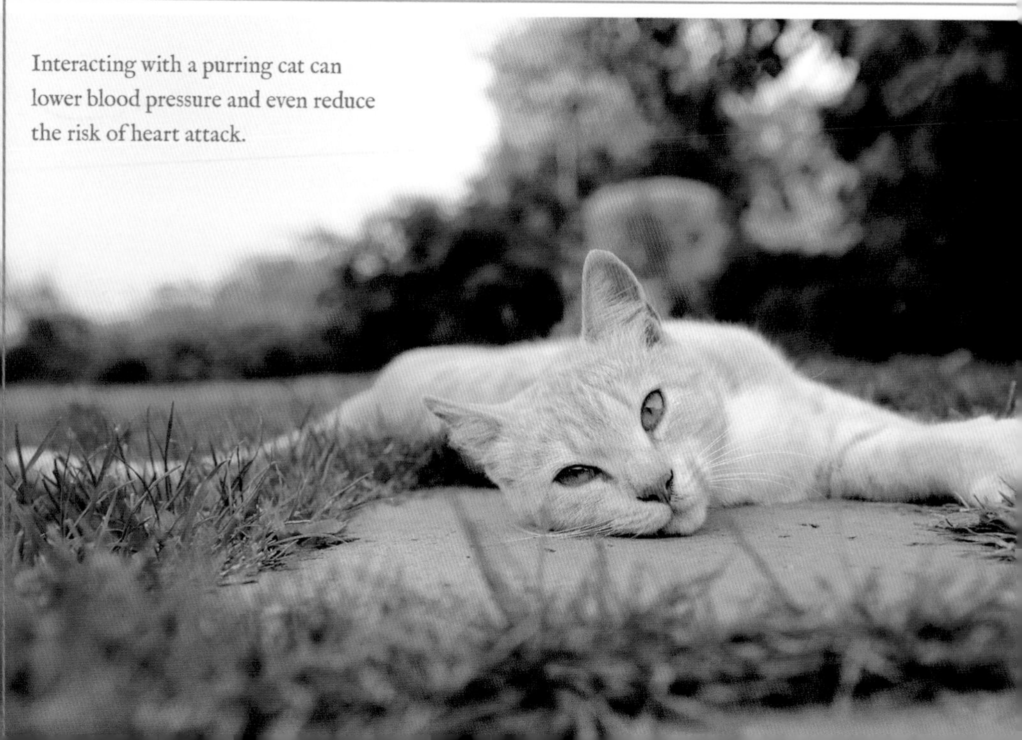

Interacting with a purring cat can lower blood pressure and even reduce the risk of heart attack.

26

Pruning Brings Growth

I am the true grapevine, and my Father is the gardener. He cuts off every branch of mine that doesn't produce fruit, and he prunes the branches that do bear fruit so they will produce even more. You have already been pruned and purified by the message I have given you. Remain in me, and I will remain in you. For a branch cannot produce fruit if it is severed from the vine, and you cannot be fruitful unless you remain in me.

JOHN 15:1-4

IN LATE WINTER, on a drive through Sonoma County, I'll see farmworkers pruning fruit trees. A few farms haven't given out to vineyard and still grow apples, peaches, cherries, apricots, and plums. In winter the view is bleak; we'll see orchards of barren-looking trees and piles of cuttings ready to burn. But why prune at all?

Pruning cuts away diseased and storm-damaged branches. It also removes obstructing branches that might otherwise break off and wound the trunk, exposing the interior of the tree to insect invasion. Pruning thins the tree's crown and branches, permitting more air to circulate and light to penetrate. Air and light are essential to flower production—and without flowers, there is no fruit. Pruning strengthens the tree for fruit production and shapes it into something of beauty.

We need pruning, too, and not just once a year. What does God use to prune us? Scripture; life experiences, both good and bad; the natural world; others' words. We learn through hardship. We learn through pain. Everything becomes a tool in God's hands.

But I have a part in the process too. God calls me to examine my life, to search for what needs to be cut away. Do I listen to the raucous shouting world instead of the still small voice of God? Cut away that part of me that desires the world's approval. Has pride crept in

"If you are going to be a fruitful Christian, you must cooperate with God's pruning in your life."
RICK WARREN

like a disease? Cut away that self-righteousness. What useless, time-consuming, needless things need to be cut away so I have the time I crave to lean in and listen to the Holy Spirit moving within my heart, instructing while I read God's Word, lighting my path through this fallen, darkened world? Whatever obstructs my relationship with God must be cut off and tossed on the burn pile.

Pruning brings new life.

I want to be strong in faith, like a tree firmly planted by streams of

living water. I want to yield fruit in season—love, joy, peace, patience, kindness, goodness, faithfulness, gentleness, self-control—because these are the things that make others hunger for the One who fills the soul.

✿ REFLECT

Why is pruning so uncomfortable? How can it help us become more fruitful? What is God's role in the process and what is ours? What new life can emerge after pruning?

✿ APPLY

Take some quiet time this week to search your heart. What areas of your life need pruning? What attitudes or thoughts need to be cut off so that you can become more fruitful?

✿ CONNECT WITH GOD

Father God, You are the master Gardener. You know how to prune me so that I will become more fruitful, more beautiful, more like You. The pruning is often painful, and I wish it weren't necessary. But please help me to remember that no matter how much it hurts in the moment, the end result will be more fruit—and a life that is an offering to You.

I used to wander off until you disciplined me;
but now I closely follow your word.

PSALM 119:67

Heeding God's Warnings

Be careful then, dear brothers and sisters. Make sure that your own hearts are not evil and unbelieving, turning you away from the living God. You must warn each other every day, while it is still "today," so that none of you will be deceived by sin and hardened against God. For if we are faithful to the end, trusting God just as firmly as when we first believed, we will share in all that belongs to Christ.

HEBREWS 3:12-14

ONE OF MY FAVORITE state parks in northern California is Goat Rock, which is on the mouth of the Russian River. Our family is familiar with this area because Rick's mom and dad lived in Jenner, a small hamlet overlooking the river and with views of the coast. If you've ever seen the movie *The Goonies,* you've seen Goat Rock.

Goat Rock offers choices. A walk north on the beach will take you to the mouth of the river, where you can watch California sea lions and their pups fishing and basking in the sun. If you drive south and park, you can walk on a sand-and-pebble beach with a view of an arched-rock island white-topped with seagulls (and their guano). Goat Rock is between the two beaches, and going in the water there

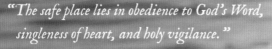

is tempting to some—but not everyone who does is lucky enough to be rescued.

Warning signs are posted. No lifeguard is on duty, and this is a hazardous place to be if you're not paying attention. The surf is powerful, and the undertow pulls you down deep where great white sharks roam. If you somehow manage to get back to the surface, there's still the riptide that pulls you out to sea. Over sixty people have been swept off their feet and disappeared.

If it's so dangerous, why do I love this park?

I like to watch the sea lions. I love the rhythm of the pounding surf,

sometimes so heavy you can feel the power in your chest. I love the pools of pebbles and myriad of colors with each wave. I love the wind in my hair and the smell of salt, sea, and sand, the sound of seagulls, and all the treasures you find along the beach.

I stay safe because I heed the warnings. My life and the lives of those I love who come with me depend upon believing what those signs tell us.

The Bible offers warnings, too. We're told to stay alert, to resist the devil (see 1 Peter 5:8), to heed the examples of others in the past (see 1 Corinthians 10:11), to keep our hearts from being hardened against God (see Hebrews 3:13). The truth is sobering: Those who mock God's existence and turn their backs on Him will fall down, be pulled under and lost. But those who take God at His Word have a future and a hope.

❊ REFLECT

Which of God's warnings do you find most difficult to heed? Why do we sometimes have a hard time listening to warnings?

❊ APPLY

Consider the Scriptures mentioned above (1 Peter 5:8; 1 Corinthians 10:11; Hebrews 3:13). What truths can you meditate on this week that will help you remember the importance of following God's warnings?

❊ CONNECT WITH GOD

Father God, teach me to see Your warnings as acts of love. Just as Danger! signs keep people out of treacherous riptides, Your limits are in place to protect me. May I always heed Your warnings and share them with others out of love.

> The laws of the LORD are true;
>   each one is fair. . . .
> They are a warning to your servant,
>   a great reward for those who obey them.
>
> PSALM 19:9, 11

28

Faithful to the End

Don't be selfish; don't try to impress others. Be humble, thinking of others as better than yourselves. Don't look out only for your own interests, but take an interest in others, too. You must have the same attitude that Christ Jesus had.

PHILIPPIANS 2:3-5

YEARS AGO, to celebrate our anniversary, my husband gave me a gold necklace with a pendant: two small golden geese flying side by side. The geese represent eternal love.

Geese mate for life. If a goose becomes too old or sick to continue in formation with the rest of the flock, the mate and another goose will fly with the weaker one between them to a place with food and water. The two will wait and comfort the weaker one until either it is able to fly or it dies. Only then will the stronger geese join another flock, where they will be welcomed as newcomers.

Geese fly in a V formation. The goose in front actually creates air movement that makes flying easier for the birds behind. When the lead bird grows weary, another moves into lead position. The oldest and youngest geese fly at the back of the V and honk like a cheering

"You don't live in a world all alone. Your brothers are here too."
ALBERT SCHWEITZER

With the right kind of wind, a V formation of Canada geese
can cover up to 1,500 miles in just twenty-four hours.

section for those ahead. By working together as a unit, these birds can fly great distances that they could never manage alone.

How much we can learn about loyalty from geese! Proverbs 17:17 reminds us that "A friend is always loyal, and a brother is born to help in time of need." We need to seek out those friends who will support us when we are weak, stick with us no matter what, and cheer us on when we step out to lead. Do we exhibit that kind of loyalty to our spouses and those close to us?

When we are committed to others' well-being—when we value them above ourselves and put their interests first, as Paul instructs the Philippians—we are imitating Jesus and taking on His mind-set. He is the ultimate faithful friend.

May we stay faithful and committed to our spouses "until death do us part." May we take turns in a leadership position and cheer one another on for the long journey ahead. And may we always welcome newcomers and the lost.

"The race of mankind would perish did they cease to aid each other. We cannot exist without mutual help."

SIR WALTER SCOTT

REFLECT

Think back over the past few years of your life. Which people have been loyal friends to you? How did they show it? Take a moment to evaluate yourself. How well do you cheer on others in their efforts or support those around you who are weak?

❈ APPLY

This week, remember God's faithfulness and strive to imitate it. Decide on one thing you can do to support a friend who is struggling right now.

❈ CONNECT WITH GOD

Lord God, You are the only One who is fully faithful. I am grateful that You will stick by me no matter what. Thank You for the people in my life who show that same kind of loyalty to me. Please help me to extend it to others too, whether it's my spouse, other family members, friends, or those around me. I want to be a reflection of You.

You, Lord, are a compassionate and gracious God,
slow to anger, abounding in love and faithfulness.

PSALM 86:15, NIV

29

Waiting on God

God has made everything beautiful for its own time. He has planted eternity in the human heart, but even so, people cannot see the whole scope of God's work from beginning to end.

ECCLESIASTES 3:11

WE HAVE A DOGWOOD TREE in our backyard. A few springs ago, all the others in the neighborhood were blooming in their pink-and-white glory. Mine was still sleeping in the corner with the oak spreading its protective arms over it.

I thought the dogwood was dead. I gave it a closer look and discovered it had new growth coming, the promise of something happening. I wanted to shake it a little and wake it up. It worked on a birch tree that Rick got tired of looking at some years ago and tried to pull up with his bare hands. He pulled and yanked and gave it a kick or two—but it wouldn't come out. The next year, it thrived. So here I was debating. Did my dogwood need some rough handling? I preferred talking: "Come on! Pretty please. Bloom! We're leaving soon on a trip and I don't want to miss your show." It snoozed on.

The friend who house-sat for me during our trip had the pleasure of the dogwood's display. She could sit on the deck with the sun shining, look down into the shady area below, and see those beautiful flowers spreading across every branch. Maybe the timing wasn't just right for me, but it was for her.

Everything happens in God's perfect time. The wise king Solomon communicated this beautifully in Ecclesiastes 3. Not only does Solomon say there is a season, or time, for "every activity under heaven," he ends with the striking statement that "God has made everything beautiful for its own time" (v. 11). What looks wrong, out of sync, or just plain ugly to us is simply unfinished to God. His plans are not yet complete. He has the ability to bring beauty out of everything—in its perfect time, which He alone determines. As Solomon says, we can't see "the whole scope of God's work from beginning to end." It's far beyond our comprehension. So our role is to wait patiently, trusting that He can make everything beautiful—even the messes of our own lives.

Sometimes the things that look dead are just getting ready to grow.

"Patient waiting is often the highest way of doing God's will."

JEREMY COLLIER

I am confident I will see the Lord's goodness
while I am here in the land of the living.

PSALM 27:13

✵ REFLECT

When have you had to wait for something? How difficult was it for you to wait for God's timing? What helps you to wait patiently?

✵ APPLY

What are you waiting for right now? Consider a situation in your life that looks ugly or even dead. What would have to happen for God to make it beautiful? Ask God for the patience to wait for His timing.

✵ CONNECT WITH GOD

Lord, You know how often I am impatient, wanting to see results right now. Forgive me for thinking that I know best. I know I can't see Your whole plan. I'm so grateful that You care enough to make everything beautiful in its time. Teach me patience as I wait.

I am confident I will see the LORD's goodness
while I am here in the land of the living.
Wait patiently for the LORD.
Be brave and courageous.
Yes, wait patiently for the LORD.

PSALM 27:13-14

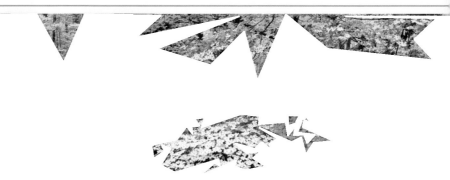

30

Unending Faithfulness

If we are unfaithful,
he remains faithful,
for he cannot deny who he is.

2 TIMOTHY 2:13

M Y FIRST of many sightings of storks took place in Segovia, Spain. While others gawked at the Roman aqueduct, I gawked at a muster of white storks (with black wings and red bills and legs) tending their hatchlings in huge nests on the tops of towers and tiled roofs. Four nests on one tower alone, and as many loving couples with young. I longed for binoculars.

Storks are reputed to be monogamous (for a season). Mating pairs return to these high nests year after year, adding to them until they weigh over a thousand pounds. How would you like that nest on your roof?

Storks have a varied diet of frogs, fish, insects, earthworms, and small birds and mammals. They are listed among the "unclean" birds in Scripture, probably because "small birds and mammals" would

Praise Him for His grace and favor
To our fathers in distress;
Praise Him, still the same forever,
Slow to chide, and swift to bless,
Alleluia! Alleluia! Glorious in His faithfulness.

"PRAISE, MY SOUL, THE KING OF HEAVEN"

include disease-carrying rats and mice. Wouldn't it be nice to have a personal rodent exterminator keeping watch from your roof? If storks lived in California, I'd want to mount a metal platform above the roof and put up a sign: Stork Building Site.

Not vastly intelligent, they are still wiser than most of us. The Lord spoke of the stork through the prophet Jeremiah: "Even the stork that flies across the sky knows the time of her migration, as do the turtledove, the swallow, and the crane. They all return at the proper time each year. But not my people! They do not know the Lord's laws" (Jeremiah 8:7).

Animals instinctively know what they were created to do, often following patterns of life and migration that go back scores of generations. Yet we humans continually forget that we are created for God's glory. He made us to have a relationship with Him, yet we turn away from Him again and again. But just as He was faithful to the Israelites, loving them and calling them His people even after they turned to idols, He is faithful to us. As 2 Timothy tells us, God "cannot deny who he is"—the faithful One. He will not go against His nature. Sometimes He shows His love through discipline to help us see clearly the desperate situation we're in, but He always calls us back.

When we repent and live in His will, we become what God created us to be. Like the storks, we'll be fulfilling our created purpose.

"God is faithful even when his children are not."

MAX LUCADO

REFLECT

What does our culture tell us is our ultimate purpose in life? In what ways do we struggle to remember our true purpose? How can we be faithful to the goal of glorifying our faithful God?

APPLY

Take time this week to reflect on God's faithfulness. Read stories from Scripture that show people's rebellion, God's discipline, and then His calling them again to Himself. (For example, the story of David and Bathsheba in 2 Samuel 11–12:25; the story of Jonah in the book of Jonah; the story of Peter's denial and reinstatement in Luke 22:31-34, 54-62 and John 21:15-19). Journal about what God's faithfulness means in your life and how you might be more faithful in maintaining a relationship with Him.

CONNECT WITH GOD

Heavenly Father, You are the faithful One. You keep on loving us even when we turn away from You over and over. It would be easy for You to walk away or even start over with a whole new creation, but Your love is steadfast. I'm so grateful that I can count on You, no matter what. Please help me to respond with faithfulness too. I don't want to waste my life; I want to live with the right purpose in mind so that I can be the person You created me to be.

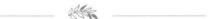

Your unfailing love, O LORD, is as vast as the heavens;
your faithfulness reaches beyond the clouds.

PSALM 36:5

31

The Miracle of Prayer

*Let us come boldly to the throne of our gracious God.
There we will receive his mercy, and we will find grace
to help us when we need it most.*

HEBREWS 4:16

RICK USED TO take customers, friends, and family members salmon fishing in Alaska and British Columbia. Before heading out in a small boat, he and his companion always checked the gear, such as nets, gaff, compass, and map.

His most memorable trip was with our eldest son, Trevor. They were so excited one morning that they jumped right in the boat and headed out. They fished, mostly catch-and-release, and cruised in and out of dozens of small inlets and bays. When they were ready to head back toward the lodge where they were staying, a dense fog bank fell upon them. It was so thick that Rick could barely see our son at the other end of the boat. He wasn't worried and reached for the compass. But for the first time in five trips north, Rick had forgotten to check for equipment. The compass and map were not in the boat.

If he put in toward shore without knowing exactly where he was, they could end up on the rocks. If he put out into the channel, he could place them in a shipping lane. Think cruise ship going over a dinghy. Rick put on a brave face and said, "Don't worry, Son. I can dead reckon back to the lodge."

After several hours of going in circles, they were filled with dread. Rick later said, "I faced the possibility that my stupidity in not checking for the compass and map might very well result in the death of my son, not to mention his dim-witted daddy." It occurred to him in that moment that he should turn the navigation over to God. So he prayed: "Father, I don't care what You do with me—this mess is my fault. But please spare my son, who trusted me to get him out and back safely!"

In that moment, God parted a curtain. The fog split fifty feet away

"I have been many times driven to my knees by the overwhelming conviction that I had nowhere else to go."
ABRAHAM LINCOLN

in bright sunshine, right at the small opening of the lodge's inlet. God had guided them home.

God's Word is clear when it directs us to pray—at all times, in all circumstances. In Hebrews 4 we're instructed to "come boldly" to God's throne. We can approach our majestic God with confidence because He has promised to respond with mercy and grace. What a blessing! Our heavenly Father is always listening, and He always cares. If you're ever lost in the fog or "in a fog," pray. You might just experience a miracle.

"None can believe how powerful prayer is, and what it is able to effect, but those who have learned it by experience."

MARTIN LUTHER

REFLECT

Why do you think God encourages us to approach Him boldly? Do you find this easy or difficult? How can you make prayer a more immediate reaction when you're faced with challenging situations?

APPLY

Make a list of the times in your life when God answered your prayer—whether in a dramatic fashion, as in Rick's story, or in a quieter, more private way. Take a moment to thank Him. Return to this list next time you need help. It will be a good reminder of God's continuing, loving care.

CONNECT WITH GOD

Lord God, You are so great, and yet You ask us to come to You with our needs and requests. Thank You for caring for me. Please help me to be persistent in prayer, even in those times when I don't see answers right away. Help me to remember all the times when You have helped me in the past and to trust in Your love and goodness for the future.

In my distress I cried out to the LORD;
yes, I prayed to my God for help.
He heard me from his sanctuary;
my cry to him reached his ears.

PSALM 18:6

32

Seeking the True Light

Jesus spoke to the people once more and said, "I am the light of the world. If you follow me, you won't have to walk in darkness, because you will have the light that leads to life."

JOHN 8:12

EVERY EVENING, moths gather outside the window of our downstairs family room. They beat against the glass, trying to get to the lamp inside. Sometimes after our dog Sarge has gone out, he stalls at the door, playing with them, and they manage to flitter inside and dash themselves against the lightbulb.

Remember the bug zappers that were once popular? The false light attracted moths and insects, electrocuting them when they came close.

People can be like moths, going after false light. The prophet Isaiah begged the Israelites not to do this: "If you are walking in darkness, without a ray of light, trust in the Lord and rely on your God. But watch out, you who live in your own light and warm yourselves by your own fires" (50:10-11). He wasn't talking about building a campfire. He was talking about rejecting God and worshiping idols—something the Israelites had been doing off and on for hundreds of years, even before they entered the Promised Land. *Idol* literally means "little nothing." An idol is not only a graven image; it is anything that replaces the living God in our lives. That could be status, family, reputation, material possessions, or anything else we hold first in our hearts and trust to improve our lives.

This world is a dark place. We need light to guide us, to get us through safely. Our problem is when we try to manufacture our own light rather than turning to the true light. Like moths, we often pursue that false light of "little nothings" until we're in danger of ending up in flames. We must learn to worship only our true Savior and Lord.

Christ is the Light of the World—the Light that illumines our daily faith walk. When we draw close to Him, we won't be burned. We'll be equipped to travel in this dark, fallen world, carrying that Christlight inside that will draw others. And ultimately, that Light "leads to life." It shows us the way to our true home, where we will forever be in the presence of Light, Christ Himself.

> *I heard the voice of Jesus say,*
> *"I am this dark world's light;*
> *Look unto Me, thy morn shall rise,*
> *And all thy day be bright."*
> *I looked to Jesus and I found*
> *In Him my star, my sun;*
> *And in that light of life I'll walk*
> *Till traveling days are done.*
>
> "I HEARD THE VOICE OF JESUS SAY"

"*Whatever man loves, that is his god.*
For he carries it in his heart; he goes about with
it night and day; he sleeps and wakes with it,
be it what it may—wealth or self, pleasure or renown."

MARTIN LUTHER

REFLECT

Why did the Israelites pursue idols instead of trusting in God? Why do we sometimes do the same thing? How can a renewed vision of Jesus as the Light of the World help us turn away from our "little nothings"?

APPLY

This week, pay attention to where you turn for comfort or guidance. Take some time to write down what you discover. What things are replacing God in your life? Commit to turning solely to Him.

CONNECT WITH GOD

Lord Jesus, You are the Light of the World. Only through You can we see where we're going. Forgive me for turning to lesser things—"little nothings"—that will never satisfy and that will lead me away from You. I want to walk in Your light that leads to life. May Your light shine inside me, and may others see it and be drawn to You.

You are the fountain of life,
the light by which we see.

PSALM 36:9

33

Uprooting Sin

When you are being tempted, do not say, "God is tempting me."
God is never tempted to do wrong, and he never tempts anyone else.
Temptation comes from our own desires, which entice us and drag
us away. These desires give birth to sinful actions. And when sin
is allowed to grow, it gives birth to death.

JAMES 1:13-15

WHERE I LIVE, Scotch broom blooms everywhere in spring. It spreads like a low thicket over pastureland, and even burning doesn't kill it. Scotch broom smells wonderful, but it's a problem when left to grow at will. Tiny seeds blow hither and yon, and soon there are sprouts along roads, in backyards, and in the "green space" meant only for native plants. If the sprout isn't removed quickly, Scotch broom will sink its roots and fan underground fingers that hold fiercely. It grows fast and vigorously, blooming like yellow fire across a hillside and casting another gazillion tiny seeds into the wind.

How like sin! It can start with a small thought, take hold, and send a mind reeling into action that brings heartache and spreads grief. Sin can look like the glittering lights of Vegas, smell like the expensive perfume of Paris, taste like a feast. Then the consequences set in. The lights go out in the morning, and you see the homeless and hungry people sleeping along the fences. The perfume smells stale and sickly. The "feast" turns sour in your stomach.

Scotch broom shows me how the tiniest seed can grow into a giant weed, and warns me that a thought can become an action leading to a habit that can destroy a life. How thankful I am that I don't have to give in to sin. First Corinthians 10:13 tells us, "God is faithful. He will not allow the temptation to be more than you can stand. When

you are tempted, he will show you a way out so that you can endure."
The master Gardener can show us how to uproot the seeds of sin in
our lives.

"Temptation is the devil looking through the keyhole.
Yielding is opening the door and inviting him in."

BILLY SUNDAY

But you offer forgiveness,
that we might learn to fear you.

REFLECT

When have you seen a small choice lead to a damaging habit? When we see sin taking root in our lives, how can we eradicate it with God's help?

APPLY

This week, consider where sin might be spreading in your life. Ask God to help you keep it from becoming rooted in you.

CONNECT WITH GOD

Father, help me to take sin seriously and remember that small choices lead to bad habits. I don't want sin to become rooted in my life! Thank You for being faithful and providing a way to escape temptation. Please give me the strength to take it.

LORD, if you kept a record of our sins,
who, O Lord, could ever survive?
But you offer forgiveness,
that we might learn to fear you.

PSALM 130:3-4

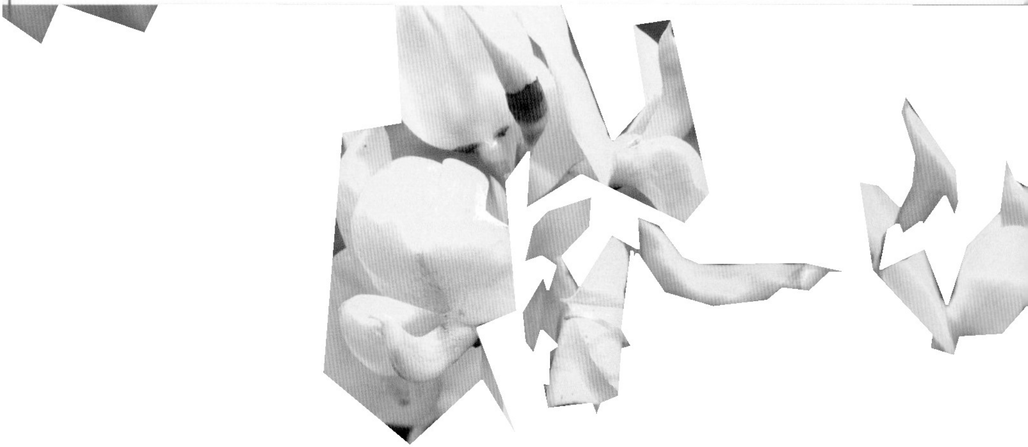

34

Encouraged to Fly

[*Jesus said,*] *"Be sure of this: I am with you always, even to the end of the age."*

MATTHEW 28:20

A RED-TAILED HAWK lives somewhere down in the green space behind our fence. We'd heard the hawk's piercing cry before but figured it was the scrub jays again, imitating the hawk's call. That high-pitched screech sends the mourning doves, quail, and songbirds scattering for cover—leaving those jays laughing as they claim our abandoned bird feeder and scarf down the seed.

This time, the piercing cries really were from hawks: not one, but three. Mom's cry sounded encouraging, mature, and confident; the babies sounded so pathetic, I wanted to weep. We kept trying to spot them, and then two perched in our tree. They weren't babies. They looked more like adolescents. And could they make noise! They'd swivel their heads and cry and cry, and Mom would answer.

I started imagining the conversation:

"Mom! We're hungry! Where's the vole?"

"You said you didn't like vole."

"What about that field mouse down there? He looks tasty."

"You've got wings. You flew to that limb, didn't you? You've got eyes! You just spotted that mouse. Go get him."

"Ah, Mooommm. We're tired. We're hungry. You do it."

"You're old enough to learn how to earn your own living."

"But we're scared, Mom. What if we crash-dive? What if we come up empty?"

"You don't think I crash-dived when I was learning? You don't think I failed? I had to learn too. Now get off your tail feathers and go for it!"

I was cheering them on. "Go for those mice! Get that rattlesnake! Come on, hawklet! Come on, hawkling! You can do it!"

Sometimes it feels like God is abandoning us to fend for ourselves. But He is always right behind us, encouraging us to do the right thing. Encouraging us when we fail. Helping us grow into the people we were meant to be. God loves us too much to let us stay where we are. He is always working for our growth, equipping us for new things and supporting us along the way. As Deuteronomy 31:8 says, "The Lord himself goes before you and will be with you; he will never leave you nor forsake you. Do not be afraid; do not be discouraged" (NIV).

Take heart, and don't be afraid to fly!

"When God speaks, oftentimes His voice will call for an act of courage on our part."

CHARLES STANLEY

The wingsp[an]
thirty-eig[ht]

❈ REFLECT

Have you ever felt that God is abandoning you? How could it change
your mind-set to consider that He might be giving you space to step
out in faith and courage? How do we know that God is always with us?

❈ APPLY

This week, identify one thing you would do if fear were not holding
you back. Ask God for the courage to try, remembering that He has
equipped you and is going before you.

❈ CONNECT WITH GOD

*Heavenly Father, so often my fear of failing keeps me from having the
courage to step out in faith. Thank You for never leaving me. Help me
to remember that You are with me every step of the way, encouraging me,
going before me, and molding me into the person You have created me to be.*

---

*The LORD is my light and my salvation—
  so why should I be afraid?
The LORD is my fortress, protecting me from danger,
  so why should I tremble?*

PSALM 27:1

35

Living by Faith

Faith shows the reality of what we hope for; it is the evidence of things we cannot see. Through their faith, the people in days of old earned a good reputation. By faith we understand that the entire universe was formed at God's command, that what we now see did not come from anything that can be seen.

HEBREWS 11:1-3

A FEW YEARS AGO, January in my area was unseasonably warm. We had blue skies, no hint of rain, and cold, frosty mornings that made way for warmer afternoons. The pruned rosebushes looked like thorny twigs. The bottlebrush still had a few blooms that fed a hummingbird. A dozen daffodils were showing their shiny yellow faces. It should have been raining, but the sky was hazy ice blue with a few wisps like downy feathers.

Sprouts were popping up all over our backyard—fooled by the warm weather into thinking it was spring. The question was, were those little sprouts basing their hope for spring on something solid enough to help them survive the possibly troubled times ahead?

Are we?

In this rush-rush, busy-busy world packed with technology and knowledge, do we look to the pundits and seemingly powerful to give us hope for the future? Or do we trust in the Lord and the power of His strength to show us the path to walk? Faith is not merely wishful thinking that makes us feel better when we're having a bad day. The writer of Hebrews tells us that faith "shows the reality of what we hope for." Another translation of that verse uses remarkably solid words to talk about an abstract concept: "Now faith is the *assurance* of things hoped for, the *conviction* of things not seen" (ESV, emphasis added). Faith is real and tangible because it is grounded in God, who is the ultimate reality.

The little sprouts in the backyard gave me a reason to pause and ask myself: *Where is my faith planted?* If I look to the world for solutions, my faith will be weak and I will wither and die. If I look to the Lord and His promises, my faith will be strong, based on what is true. He will cause me to grow even in the hardest of circumstances.

This little sprout chooses Jesus. Today and tomorrow and always, one day at a time, I choose to live by faith.

❧ REFLECT

In our culture we often view faith as nebulous and lacking substance. How does the Bible's definition differ from our culture's? How can biblical faith sustain us when trouble comes?

"I have learned that faith means trusting in advance what will make sense only in reverse."

<small>PHILIP YANCEY</small>

✠ APPLY

Think about how you might deepen your faith in God. What spiritual disciplines could help? Are there people in your life whose experiences might encourage you?

✠ CONNECT WITH GOD

Lord God, I want my faith to be strong and based on You. Help me each day to choose to live by faith. I can't always trust the things I see; things in this life won't last. May I put my trust in You—the only One who is eternal, and rock-solid, and good.

The LORD is my strength and shield.
I trust him with all my heart.
He helps me, and my heart is filled with joy.
I burst out in songs of thanksgiving.

PSALM 28:7

36

True Friendship

There are "friends" who destroy each other,
but a real friend sticks closer than a brother.

PROVERBS 18:24

THE CRAB SPIDER is an unusual arachnid. It doesn't rely on a web to catch prey. Instead, it hides in a flower and waits for a honeybee, beetle, or butterfly to come by searching for nectar. Then it pounces, grabbing the insect with its forelegs and biting it. A powerful venom does the rest.

But insects don't make up all of its diet. The males of some species of crab spiders also sip on nectar and eat pollen. Think about that. Both the crab spider and the honeybee drink the same nectar. The honeybee makes honey. The crab spider makes poison.

The same is true of people. We all breathe air and drink water. We have some of the same experiences, but what we do with them, or what we "produce," can be dramatically different.

Some people are eager to gain wisdom. They apply what they learn

The egg sac of a crab spider can contain up to 350 eggs.

to their everyday lives, including their relationships. When they see others going through difficult times, they offer practical help. They pray, send notes of support, visit, and share the struggle. They are careful with their words, speaking truth and encouragement. Like the bee, these people produce honey.

And then there are others who think they already know everything they need to know. They don't bother seeking God's wisdom. They are consumed with their own desires, and they don't really care what happens to anyone else. Sometimes they initiate conversation and seem friendly, but they're really gleaning tidbits of gossip to spread around and things to criticize—all in all causing immeasurable harm. These "crab spiders" produce poison.

You find honeybees and crab spiders in school, in the office, in church.

My mother gave me sound advice about making friends: Take time to observe the behavior of others before building friendships. Sometimes the people who greet you first are not the ones who will make the most trustworthy friends. Be polite, but watch carefully how people treat one another before establishing a friendship. Avoid the so-called friends who destroy each other, as Proverbs 18:24 says, and seek a true friend who will stick closer than a brother.

Avoid the crab spiders. Seek out the honeybees.

"The true friend seeks to give, not to take; to help, not to be helped; to minister, not to be ministered unto."

WILLIAM RADER

REFLECT

When in your life have you experienced "poison" from someone who spread gossip or criticism? Why is this behavior so harmful? How have other friends offered "honey," encouraging you or providing practical help when you needed it?

APPLY

This week, be aware of your own actions and consider how you might be a better friend, spreading honey rather than poison. What is one way you could reach out to someone else with support or encouragement?

CONNECT WITH GOD

Lord God, please guard my heart and my tongue and help me to bring good things to others with my words and actions. Give me wisdom, too, as I try to find friends who will build me up and bring me closer to You. Thank You for the gift of friendship.

Who may worship in your sanctuary, LORD?
Who may enter your presence on your holy hill?
Those who lead blameless lives and do what is right,
speaking the truth from sincere hearts.
Those who refuse to gossip
or harm their neighbors
or speak evil of their friends.

PSALM 15:1-3

37

Living Water

Jesus replied, "Anyone who drinks this water will soon become thirsty again. But those who drink the water I give will never be thirsty again. It becomes a fresh, bubbling spring within them, giving them eternal life."

JOHN 4:13-14

WHEN WE VISITED TEXAS in March a few years ago, the ground was covered with what I call "God green." We see it in the California hills in the spring too. This green is unique and can't be brought about by any human effort. People can water their gardens, irrigate their land and crops, or have expensive, high-tech sprinkler systems covering park lawns, yet never be able to re-create this color. It only happens after God sends rain. And it arrives quickly, sometimes overnight. It has an inner, almost-radiant brilliance to it.

The rain that brings about this miraculous, vibrant color reminds me of the living water Jesus talked about—water that can create a remarkable transformation in our lives.

Jesus talked about living water when He met a Samaritan woman at the well. An outcast in her own town, she was alone at the well in the heat of the day. As she and Jesus conversed about getting a drink, Jesus told her that living water would satisfy her thirst (see John 4). He was speaking not of our physical need for liquid but of our soul's deep thirst for a relationship with our Creator. No amount of struggle or work or human effort will ever satisfy that thirst—only Jesus, the living water. When we ask Him into our hearts, He fills us with the Holy Spirit, satisfying us with Himself. The Spirit transforms us into new, redeemed creations.

God splashes evidence of Himself with each rain, painting the hillsides with new life. Even those in the cities can see it in the parks and in the grass that sprouts between the cracks of concrete. When we drink the living water—when our souls are satisfied with God and we are made new creations by the Spirit—others will see evidence of our new life as well.

"Grace is the work of the Holy Spirit in transforming our desires so that knowing Jesus becomes sweeter than illicit sex, sweeter than money and what it can buy, sweeter than every fruitless joy. Grace is God satisfying our souls with his Son so that we're ruined for anything else!"

SAM STORMS

✵ REFLECT

What does it mean to be filled with living water? How can our relationship with God refresh us and transform us? What evidence of God's transformation do you think others see in your life?

My soul thirsts for you;
my whole body longs for you.

PSALM 63:1

APPLY

This week, keep in your mind the image of grass changing from dull brown to vibrant green. That's the kind of transformation the Holy Spirit can make in your life. Trust in His work.

CONNECT WITH GOD

Lord Jesus, thank You for giving Yourself as living water. You satisfy my deep thirst for a relationship with You. Teach me never to reach for anything else to quench my thirst. Thank You for working your transformation in my life. May the changes You're making help others see You in me.

O God, you are my God;
I earnestly search for you.
My soul thirsts for you;
my whole body longs for you
in this parched and weary land
where there is no water.

PSALM 63:1

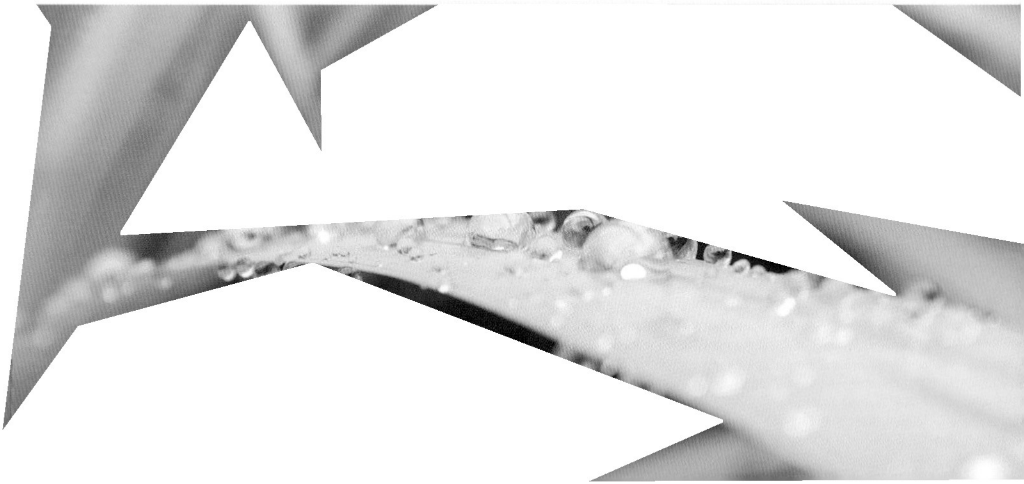

38

Rejecting Evil, Embracing Good

*Fix your thoughts on what is true, and honorable, and right, and pure,
and lovely, and admirable. Think about things that are excellent and
worthy of praise. Keep putting into practice all you learned and received
from me—everything you heard from me and saw me doing. Then the
God of peace will be with you.*

PHILIPPIANS 4:8-9

GOPHERS LIVE UNDERGROUND in tunnels. They pull
down anything edible—agricultural crops, backyard vegetable gardens, and landscaping. We have firsthand knowledge: One
gopher has managed to dig a maze of furrows all through our backyard, though he hasn't succeeded in getting into our vegetable boxes,
where I've planted bulbs. We have a thick screen underneath to keep
him out.

Gopher holes can destroy a school playing field, a lawn, a golf
course. Gophers helped drive the Russians out of Fort Ross on the
California coast in the 1840s. Their horses couldn't gallop over fields
pocked by gopher holes without risking injury to horse and rider.
Gophers also feasted on field crops and gardens. Not a beet left for
borscht.

Gophers use their teeth and front paws to
push dirt out of a tunnel onto the grass above.
Gophers do not like to share space, so each
one builds its own system of tunnels.

The gopher reminds me of other things that pull down what is good under cover of darkness. Doubts and fears pull down faith. Pride eats away at humility. Bitterness wears down hope. Gossip destroys reputations and makes our hearts hard toward others. Unholy philosophies that deny the existence of God erode our trust. Traditions and rules that replace the gospel of Jesus Christ take away the joy of salvation. All these things can destroy our peace in Christ, pulling us away from Him and toward the secular mind-set of the world around us.

First Thessalonians 5:21-22 tells us to "hold on to what is good, reject every kind of evil" (NIV). When we recognize that we're being influenced by thoughts or attitudes that weaken our faith, we need to take action to reject what is wrong. Philippians 4:8 reminds us how to go on the offensive: by filling our minds with things that are good and right and holy, excellent and praiseworthy. And the culmination of all those traits is Jesus Himself. When we fix our thoughts on Jesus, on His love and compassion and truth, on His glorious creation that exhibits His care for us—then we'll be free from those negative attitudes, and our faith will grow.

Watch out for gophers!

"All that is good, all that is true, all that is beautiful, all that is beneficent, be it great or small, be it perfect or fragmentary, natural as well as supernatural, moral as well as material, comes from God."

JOHN HENRY NEWMAN

REFLECT

What attitudes or habits pull you toward the world and away from God? How do they erode your peace in Christ? What positive, praiseworthy things can you focus on to change your perspective?

APPLY

Consider memorizing Philippians 4:8. When you sense yourself being pulled into bitterness, gossip, doubt, or other attitudes that weaken your faith, take a minute to focus on what is good and right. You'll see your perspective change.

CONNECT WITH GOD

Lord God, thank You that You are holy and right and true. Please guard me from sins and attitudes that would pull me away from You. It's easy to think the way the world thinks, but You ask us to take on Your perspective instead. Help me to turn from what is harmful, holding tight to Your righteousness and Your cleansing forgiveness.

Put your hope in the LORD.
Travel steadily along his path.

PSALM 37:34

39

Anchored in Christ

I pray that you, being rooted and established in love, may have power,
together with all the Lord's holy people, to grasp how wide and long and
high and deep is the love of Christ, and to know this love that surpasses
knowledge—that you may be filled to the measure of all the fullness of God.

EPHESIANS 3:17-19, NIV

ROOTS ANCHOR A PLANT. They draw water and nutrients from the soil and store them, and they also transport those elements to the plant's leaves so that photosynthesis can occur. The looser the soil, the more the root system can spread, improving the plant's performance and ability to survive during a dry season. As the roots grow, they have a greater capacity to absorb water, oxygen, and nutrients from the soil. In the desert, some plants have roots that are extremely deep so they can absorb water far from the dry surface. A South African evergreen called Shepherd's tree grows in the Kalahari Desert and can have roots up to sixty-eight meters deep.

In the parable of the sower (see Matthew 13), Jesus told a story about seed that was scattered on the ground. Some fell on the path and was snatched up by birds, while some fell among thorns and was soon choked by weeds. Other seed fell on rocky places with little soil, and at first it grew quickly. But when the sun beat down, the little plants withered because they had shallow roots or no roots at all—no way to receive life-giving water. Only the seeds that fell in good soil were able to take full root and grow.

As Christians, how do we keep from withering? How do we become the seed that produces a crop? We do it by putting down roots. In Ephesians 3:17-19, Paul reminded believers that Christ was living in their hearts through faith, and that God had "rooted and established" them in His love. It was only through those deepening roots that they could have any understanding of the immensity of that love and what it meant for them. The same is true for us. Only by being rooted in Christ—connected at our very core, knowing we cannot survive without Him—can we begin to grasp who He is and what He is like.

When we live in Him, study His Word, and pattern our lives after His, we receive all the "nutrients" we need to grow. We are built up and strengthened. His living water sustains and instructs us. And as time goes by, we become more firmly entrenched in Him, so that we can endure whatever comes. We are evergreen.

O the deep, deep love of Jesus!
Vast, unmeasured, boundless, free!
Rolling as a mighty ocean
In its fullness over me,
Underneath me, all around me,
Is the current of Thy love;
Leading onward, leading homeward
To my glorious rest above.

"O THE DEEP, DEEP LOVE OF JESUS!"

"Well and good if all things change,
O Lord God, provided I am rooted in You."
JOHN OF THE CROSS

The Shepherd's tree, often

✻ REFLECT

How deep are your roots in Christ? Think about the way you reacted last time you faced a crisis. How did your faith hold up? What could you do, what do you need to change, to grow deeper in Him?

✻ APPLY

This week, remember that you are rooted in Christ. He will give you everything you need.

✻ CONNECT WITH GOD

Lord Jesus, thank You that I am rooted and established in You. You are building me up, strengthening me, and helping me grow. Help me to seek to deepen my roots in You every day.

Blessed is the one
who does not walk in step with the wicked
or stand in the way that sinners take
or sit in the company of mockers,
but whose delight is in the law of the LORD,
and who meditates on his law day and night.
That person is like a tree planted by streams of water,
which yields its fruit in season
and whose leaf does not wither—
whatever they do prospers.

PSALM 1:1-3, NIV

40

Fed by God's Word

*All Scripture is inspired by God and is useful to teach us what is true
and to make us realize what is wrong in our lives. It corrects us when
we are wrong and teaches us to do what is right. God uses it to prepare
and equip his people to do every good work.*

2 TIMOTHY 3:16-17

DURING A BUS TOUR along the coast of Spain a few years
ago, our guide told us to watch for flamingos. I searched the
landscape and saw nothing but a flock of white, long-legged birds in
the distance. They looked like the egrets we have around Sonoma
County, which stand like elegant, slender statues along the roads as
they watch for frogs or lizards to come close enough to snatch in their
spear-like beaks.

Well, those white, long-legged birds in the distance were flamingos. They weren't at all like the bright-pink birds I've seen in zoos
or the plastic version someone might buy to stick on the front lawn.
Why? Because flamingos are what they eat. While most flamingos
eat (pink) shrimp, these lovely white flamingos dined on small fish
and frogs.

That got me thinking. We are what we eat, too.

When we eat junk food, we often lack energy because we're not giving ourselves the best fuel. The same is true of what we feed ourselves spiritually. What do we read and watch and listen to? Whose ideas influence our thinking? What's the first thing on our minds when we wake up, or the last thing we think about before we go to sleep? We have choices about what we focus on each day, and those choices affect us deeply.

Scripture is clear that the Word of God is powerful. Second Timothy 3 tells us that Scripture can teach us truth and help us discern what we need to change in our lives. It turns us in the right direction and prepares us for the service God has in store for us. What a wonderful gift!

When we dine on God's Word, we are being transformed into the likeness of Jesus Christ. As we nourish ourselves in the Scriptures, we're filling ourselves up with His truth and learning how to live a life that pleases Him. And just as the flamingos' diet has a visible effect that's evident to all who see them, saturating ourselves in God's Word will change the way others see us, too—because they will see Him shining through.

"The Word of God hidden in the heart
is a stubborn voice to suppress."
BILLY GRAHAM

REFLECT

If you've studied God's Word in the past, in what ways do you think it has changed you? What patterns could you modify in your daily schedule to dine on more of God's Word?

APPLY

This week, choose a passage to read and meditate on each day. (A few options: 1 John 1:8-9; Psalm 139:23-24; Philippians 4:6-8.) Consider memorizing it—"hiding it in your heart"—so that it will return to your mind in difficult moments.

CONNECT WITH GOD

Lord God, forgive me for listening too closely to other voices when I have Your very Word in front of me. May I always remember that I am affected by what I feed my mind and heart. Thank You for giving me Your powerful Word, which can teach me, change me, and equip me.

*I have hidden your word in my heart,
that I might not sin against you.*

PSALM 119:11

41

Designed by God

For the foolishness of God is wiser than human wisdom, and the
weakness of God is stronger than human strength.

1 CORINTHIANS 1:25, NIV

EVEN WITH THE PLETHORA of gorgeous vegetables in all colors available at our grocery store, Rick and I tend to call in an order at Mary's Pizza Shack or fall back on meat and potatoes.

Potatoes deserve respect. God created an original potato wild in the Andes Mountains, where enterprising Incas developed varieties in numerous colors, sizes, and textures, each able to grow in a different, often-difficult environment. Think high altitude and rocky soil! Some potatoes were bitter, some sweet, some starchy, some buttery.

After the Spanish began colonizing South America, an unknown Spaniard tossed a bag of potatoes in the hull of his ship and crossed the Atlantic to return home. The potato eventually spread to other parts of Europe, but rumors circulated that this relative of the nightshade plant was poisonous, that it would cause leprosy and immorality.

Ignoring the fears, the Irish planted the potato and thrived on it. We now know God packed potatoes with protein, as well as vitamins B6 and C.

When grain crops failed, European monarchs took another look at the lowly potato. Prussia's King Frederick the Great ordered his subjects to plant them. When that didn't work, the wily king planted them in a royal field and put guards around them, convincing his subjects that these tubers must be worth their weight in gold! Burglars snuck in by night to steal them, and soon the masses were growing them throughout the country.

Then along came an airborne fungus, probably in the belly of another ship: *Phytophthora infestans*, which made the potatoes turn black and slimy. Famine spread, and the Irish were hardest hit, both

"The higher the mountains, the more understandable is the glory of Him who made them and who holds them in His hand."
FRANCIS A. SCHAEFFER

because the potato was their main source of food and because they relied heavily on one variety of potato.

How was the fungus problem solved? Scientists went back to the Andes Mountains of South America to gather some of the original varieties of potato. They went back to the source: a disease-resistant tuber packed with nutrients to keep body and mind healthy, a plant that could grow almost anywhere and feed the multitudes. God's original design.

When we are facing a seemingly insurmountable problem that we don't know how to fix, we can turn to God's original design. He created the world with care, wisely determining how things will function best. He created and said it was good, and as 1 Corinthians 1:25 says, the best of our wisdom is no match for Him. His design is our guide.

REFLECT

In what ways does our culture deviate from God's design, and how does that affect us? Why do we think that our way is better than God's? How can we know that God's design is good?

APPLY

Take a moment to identify a challenge or decision you are facing. How might considering God's original design for people, relationships, and connection with Him help you?

CONNECT WITH GOD

Lord, I praise You for Your incredible, deliberate creation. Your design is better than the best humans could ever create. Help me to have the humility to acknowledge that You know better than I. When I'm not sure what to do, teach me to trust Your design for life.

*You made all the delicate, inner parts of my body
and knit me together in my mother's womb.
Thank you for making me so wonderfully complex!
Your workmanship is marvelous—how well I
know it.*

PSALM 139:13-14

42

The Power of Two

Let us consider how we may spur one another on toward love and good deeds, not giving up meeting together, as some are in the habit of doing, but encouraging one another—and all the more as you see the Day approaching.

HEBREWS 10:24-25, NIV

O N THE DRIVE HOME one afternoon, I spotted two large horses in a field. The animals stood parallel to one another, each one's head to the other's tail end. Tails swished as they kept annoying flies away from the other's face. The constant buzzing of flies must be a great irritation—but it's more than just a nuisance. If given time and opportunity, flies can deposit bacteria, larvae, and parasites in the horses' eyes. These two horses worked as a team to protect one another.

In Luke 10 we read that Jesus sent seventy-two of His followers out two by two to go ahead of Him, healing the sick and preaching about the coming Kingdom of God. Why in pairs? He knew that a man or woman alone is vulnerable. Loneliness, doubts, and a constant barrage of hostile questions and false truths can be like the buzzing of a thousand flies. When we're on our own, those things distract us and even threaten our well-being. But when we pair with others, we can offer encouragement. We can remind one another of what Jesus taught and what Scripture says. We can uphold one another through hardship and heartache, knowing that God loves us and will never abandon us. We can challenge each other to look for new ways to love

"Aloneness can lead to loneliness. God's preventative for loneliness is intimacy—meaningful, open, sharing relationships with one another. In Christ we have the capacity for the fulfilling sense of belonging which comes from intimate fellowship with God and with other believers."

NEIL T. ANDERSON

and serve those around us. These are all ways to, as Hebrews 10 says, "spur one another on toward love and good deeds."

May we take a lesson from these horses and recognize the great benefit that comes from partnering with other believers—for accountability, for encouragement, and for support as we seek to do the work the Lord has set before us.

REFLECT

Are you facing struggles that you're attempting to handle on your own? How might partnering with another believer encourage you and help you to escape temptations and doubts?

APPLY

Think of one new ministry or act of service you have been nervous to try on your own. Consider whose partnership might bring you the accountability and encouragement you need.

CONNECT WITH GOD

Lord Jesus, thank You for all the times the believers around me have supported me in my troubles and challenged me to follow You more wholeheartedly. I'm grateful for the gift of community.

I will proclaim your name to my brothers and sisters.
I will praise you among your assembled people.

PSALM 22:22

Because horses' eyes are on the sides of their heads, they have an almost 360-degree range of vision.

43

Letting God Be the Judge

Do not judge others, and you will not be judged. For you will be treated as you treat others. The standard you use in judging is the standard by which you will be judged.

MATTHEW 7:1-2

ON OUR TRIP to Alaska we saw both glaciers (large masses of ice that move across land) and icebergs (pieces of glacier floating in the ocean). It was an amazing thing to watch a glacier calve, or break off, sections into the sea. We watched with some trepidation as the chunks floated toward our boat. As one chunk came toward us, a piece of jutting white ice shone above the surface. The closer the iceberg came, the more visible the rock-hard, jagged-edged steel blue glowed beneath. Those edges were large and sharp enough to slice open the side of a ship. (The *Titanic* came to mind, though I try not to think about a sinking ocean liner when I'm aboard one.)

Here's the truth about icebergs: No matter how much ice we see above the waterline, the biggest part of the iceberg is hidden beneath the ocean.

People are like icebergs. We see a part of them, but the real

Seven-eighths of an iceberg's mass is under the water.

person—the whole person—is hidden below the surface. Still waters run deep, the saying goes. In fact, all human beings run deep. Only God knows what they have experienced; what troubles they have faced or are still facing; what they think about; what dreams and hopes they have; what pain, what joy, what good and evil they have encountered.

In the Sermon on the Mount, Jesus tells us not to judge one another. One simple reason is because we're not equipped to do it well. We see or hear only what's on the surface of a person's life; we don't understand his or her thoughts or motivations. God alone sees the heart, the mind, the soul hidden within each human being. He who made our innermost parts knows our innermost hearts.

Of course we have to decide which people we will trust and invest in, so we sometimes need to draw conclusions about others based on their actions. But we must always do that in humility, remembering that we don't have the whole picture about anyone. Nor does anyone else have the whole picture about us. Thank God that He alone, who is holy and righteous, can and will judge.

"Man measures everything by his own experience; he has no other yardstick."

DOROTHY SAYERS

REFLECT

Think about a time when you felt unfairly judged for something you did or said. How did you react? How can you avoid making those same imperfect judgments about others and develop more grace in your approach to those around you?

APPLY

Think of one person in your life whom you tend to judge because you assume you know his or her thoughts or motivations. Take a minute to give the other person the benefit of the doubt by imagining a different, better motivation. How might that mind-set change the way you approach him or her?

CONNECT WITH GOD

Father, You know that I am often tempted to judge others. I hear one unkind word and deem someone unkind. I see one impatient look and label someone impatient. Forgive me for forgetting that all people consist of far more than I can see or hear. I am grateful that You know me—and all people—fully. You alone are a just judge, and Your decisions are always right. Please help me to leave the judging to You and instead respond to people around me with compassion.

O LORD, you have examined my heart
and know everything about me.
You know when I sit down or stand up.
You know my thoughts even when I'm far away.

PSALM 139:1-2

44

Laying Aside Worry

*Don't worry about these things, saying, "What will we eat? What will
we drink? What will we wear?" These things dominate the thoughts
of unbelievers, but your heavenly Father already knows all your needs.
Seek the Kingdom of God above all else, and live righteously, and he
will give you everything you need.*

MATTHEW 6:31-33

YEARS AGO Rick and I visited the Alhambra, a castle and
fortress in Granada, Spain. While exploring the medieval
buildings, I spotted birds swooping into the courtyard and diving
into the lacy arabesques on archways and walls. The Alhambra is a
masterpiece of Moorish architecture described by poets as "a pearl set
in emeralds"—the pale palace complex surrounded by vibrant green
myrtle and orange trees inhabited by nightingales. Bits of straw and
mud peeped out of these magnificent palace structures. More swifts
dipped and soared, diving into their hidden nests to feed their young.
It reminded me of Proverbs 30:28, which speaks of lizards living even
in royal palaces.

Swallows also make their homes in unexpected places. Plain birds
with long wings, they maneuver like fighter pilots for a beak full of

mud to build their tidy nests. In California, "swallow apartments" line the underbellies of overpasses along Interstate 5. Other swallows tuck their mud nests tightly beneath eaves of houses or in historic Jesuit missions.

Jesus' words come like a whisper as I watch these birds: "Look at the birds of the air: they neither sow nor reap nor gather into barns, and yet your heavenly Father feeds them. Are you not of more value than they?" (Matthew 6:26, ESV).

Jesus tells us that we don't have to spend all our waking moments focused on the daily details of life, the here and now of food and shelter and clothing. That's true whether we're worried about having enough or about having the right kind. We don't have to live as if no one is looking out for us, because God is looking out for us. He knows when a swallow falls. He knows how many hairs we have on our heads. He cares about the details of our lives.

When we focus first on our worries, that's all we have room for. But when we focus first on God and His Kingdom, seeking it above all else as Jesus instructs, we'll find that our worries begin to fade. We'll

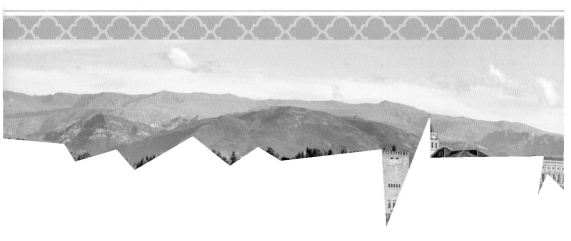

gain perspective and realize that we can trust Him to care for us. We can rest in the knowledge that the Lord who tucks swifts into palaces and provides food for them will never abandon His children.

❊ REFLECT

What day-to-day worries fill your mind and sap your trust? When do you find it most difficult to trust in God? What do you think it means to "seek the Kingdom of God above all else"? Take a few moments to go outside and watch the birds. How can birds or other animals in nature encourage you to remember that God cares deeply for your everyday needs?

❊ APPLY

Write Matthew 6:31-33 on an index card or Post-it note and put it in a place where you'll see it each day (on your bathroom mirror, on your computer, on your car's dashboard, or typed into your phone).

The Alhambra is home to more than 150 species of wildlife, some permanent and some seasonal.

Lord God, it's so easy for me to get caught up in worrying about day-to-day things: What I'm going to wear or eat. My home. Sometimes I'm worried about having enough, and sometimes I worry about having the right things. Help me to remember that these possessions are not my top priority. You are. Your Kingdom is. I know I can only focus on it when I remember that I can trust You with my daily needs. Thank You for caring for me.

I know every bird on the mountains,
and all the animals of the field are mine.

PSALM 50:11

"Worry does not empty tomorrow of its sorrows;
it empties today of its strength."

CORRIE TEN BOOM

Swallows construct nests out of mud pellets they hold in their beaks. Nests are usually shaped like cups or gourds, and the insides are lined with grass, hair, or feathers.

45

Strength through Struggle

We can rejoice, too, when we run into problems and trials, for we know that they help us develop endurance. And endurance develops strength of character, and character strengthens our confident hope of salvation.

ROMANS 5:3-4

ON A TRIP to a local butterfly garden, my two granddaughters and I followed instructions and stayed on the paths, didn't pick plants, and refrained from picking up caterpillars. As we strolled among the butterfly bushes, verbena, pincushion flowers and asters, the plantain, grasses, and milkweeds, we spotted a "mock" monarch, a pipevine swallowtail, a cabbage white, a yellow-and-black western tiger swallowtail, and a dozen or more black-and-orange swallowtail caterpillars dining on the Dutchman's-pipe vine.

I had a lot to learn about these beautiful insects. Some interesting tidbits about butterfly behavior: They go "nectaring," dipping their long tubular tongues into a flower to eat. They also dine on rotten fruit and animal droppings, and they "puddle," or sip, dissolved minerals and salts from wet earth. The males "hilltop" by finding a high spot where they patrol and defend their territory while seeking a mate. Females oviposit, or lay eggs singly or in clutches on specific host plants (like the Dutchman's-pipe vine). Butterflies also bask in the sunshine to warm their cold-blooded bodies.

Maybe you've heard the story about a child who thought he was helping a butterfly by splitting open its cocoon so the creature could escape more easily. Without the struggle to get out, though, the butterfly's wings didn't develop the strength needed to fly.

Sometimes an act of mercy can get in the way of God's blessings. Whether I want to jump in and help someone else, or I want someone to rescue me, I've learned the hard way this can cause more harm than good. The uncomfortable truth is that trials and tribulations are often training grounds for great growth in character and in faith. Romans 5 tells us that problems build our ability to persevere through struggle, even if we can't see the end point. That endurance in turn develops our character, which is the core of who we are even when no one is observing us, and then "strengthens our confident hope of salvation." And that's really the key, isn't it? That kind of hope—trusting that God really is redeeming us, that He really has a glorious eternal future planned for us—changes everything.

Sometimes God does step in and rescue us. But often it's when we struggle that we turn to Him for help and discover the immensity and beauty of His tender care. Only then can we mount up on wings of faith and fly.

"We are always in the forge, or on the anvil;
by trials God is shaping us for higher things."
HENRY WARD BEECHER

Your promise revives me;
it comforts me in
all my Troubles.
PSALM 119:50

There are approximately 20,000 species
of butterflies in the world! More than 700
of them have been seen in North America.

✖ REFLECT

Think back on a time when you wished God would step in and change your circumstances, but instead you had to struggle through a problem. Do you think your faith and character were strengthened as a result? How? If not, what do you think stood in the way of that change?

✖ APPLY

This week, ask God to help you view trials as an opportunity to grow.

✖ CONNECT WITH GOD

Lord, often I just want my troubles to go away. But I know that You are sovereign, and You have a purpose for what I experience. Please don't let these struggles be wasted. May my trials create in me endurance, character, faith, and an unshakable hope in the salvation that comes only from You.

Your promise revives me;
it comforts me in all my troubles.

PSALM 119:50

46

Trusting God's Provision

*God will generously provide all you need. Then you will always have
everything you need and plenty left over to share with others.*

2 CORINTHIANS 9:8

OUR BIRD FEEDER provides both great entertainment and
timely lessons. One morning, my grandchildren observed a
"bully" blue jay that pecked and chased away smaller birds so he could
hog the feeder. When the jay is away, several varieties of songbirds
will feast happily together. The blue jay, however, wants all the food
for himself—plus possibly one bully buddy. One day I put out peanuts
for the squirrel, and two jays cleaned out the entire bowl in five minutes, taking turns stashing the nuts in the woods below our house.

This isn't the only bully jay I've known. In a previous home, we
had a shelf outside the kitchen window on which I scattered seed so I
could have an up close and personal look at birds in our yard. The jay
took over the shelf. When he finished off the seed, he looked at me
through the window with raised (or seemingly so) white brows. He'd
tilt his head and glare. I could almost hear his thoughts: "Give me
some more." When I didn't oblige, he pecked the window.

"*The world says, the more you take, the more you have.*
Christ says, the more you give, the more you are."

FREDERICK BUECHNER

We shouldn't allow bullying. We need to catch it early and stop it before it becomes a bad habit—or criminal behavior.

My grandchildren were upset at the jay's bullying behavior that morning. Since I was busy making sausage and pancakes, I sent my grandson out with a spray bottle that shoots a straight, strong stream of water. My grandson is a very good shot. I could almost hear the songbirds singing praise, and then one by one they returned to feast happily together.

The blue jay shows what selfishness looks like. There is plenty of seed for all the birds, but he has an attitude of "I don't want a share. I want it all!" But for what purpose? When he and his bully buddy took all the peanuts, they stored their plunder in treasure warehouses in the woods where the peanuts will rot long before they're eaten. That's not unlike many people who put their time and effort into accumulating material things that will only lose value and decay.

The apostle Paul reminds us that God will provide all that we need. If we know that, we can be content with what we have instead of always seeking more. We can live in generosity instead of selfishness. Just like the chickadees and finches, who take turns on the perches and sometimes feast around the base together. They receive enough, enjoy what was provided, and fly away satisfied. A good lesson for us to learn.

✖ REFLECT

How does our culture encourage selfishness? Why do we sometimes want not just enough but more than everyone else? How does it change our attitude when we trust that God will provide for us?

APPLY

This week, think about one way you can be generous with others. Perhaps it's sending a gift card to a family who is struggling financially, offering to bring a meal to a friend who is sick, or volunteering your time to help a disabled person complete a chore that's physically difficult for him or her. Ask God to refresh you through your act of generosity (see Proverbs 11:25).

CONNECT WITH GOD

Lord God, forgive me for my lack of generosity. I know much of it comes from my fear of not having enough. Please help me to trust completely in Your promise to provide for me physically and emotionally. I don't have to fight for what's mine, because You will give me what I need. Teach me to have open hands and to give generously from what You have given me.

How joyful are those who fear the LORD
and delight in obeying his commands. . . .
They share freely and give generously to those in need.
Their good deeds will be remembered forever.
They will have influence and honor.

PSALM 112:1, 9

47

Rescued from Sin

Give us today the food we need,
and forgive us our sins,
*   as we have forgiven those who sin against us.*
And don't let us yield to temptation,
*   but rescue us from the evil one.*

MATTHEW 6:11-13

CARNIVOROUS PLANTS may sound like an oxymoron, but they exist—and the Venus flytrap is probably the best known. These plants can survive in imperfect conditions because they don't rely completely on the soil for their nutrients. Their secondary source of food? Insects.

Pairs of the Venus flytrap's leaves form "jaws" that rest partly closed. Where the leaves join is a series of tiny trigger hairs. If an insect touches two hairs in a row, the leaves will close, trapping the bug inside and slowly dissolving it with digestive acid. Once the insect is digested, the leaves will open again, ready for a new victim.

The Venus flytrap presents a picture of how temptation and sin work together. The plant wouldn't survive without a way to attract insects, so it produces a sweet, sticky nectar that looks so good and promises so much. In the same way, temptation looks beautiful, sweet, fun, rewarding. It lures us into sin, which captures us and holds us prisoner. Like flies, we enter into temptation to sip the sweetness we thought was there and find ourselves stuck, sinking into acid that dissolves our character and devours our lives.

The Venus flytrap is beautiful—a stunning creation of God. Satan makes sin look beautiful, too, until we give in to it and then see it for what it really is. We must remember that Satan is a liar and a murderer who will never change (see John 8:44). He hates God and stabs at the heart of heaven by fooling, corrupting, and taking His children captive.

Look to Jesus. He is Truth. When we cry out to Him, He rescues us. He has washed away the sickening sweetness of sin and indwelt us with His Holy Spirit so we can resist the traps Satan sets for us. As Colossians 1:13-14 tells us, we are no longer part of the kingdom of darkness but are in His Kingdom. We are forgiven. While we need to be alert, we don't need to fear Satan's traps anymore. We can fly free.

Out of my bondage, sorrow and night,
Jesus, I come, Jesus, I come;
Into Thy freedom, gladness and light,
Jesus, I come to Thee;
Out of my sickness into Thy health,
out of my want and into Thy wealth,
Out of my sin and into Thyself,
Jesus, I come to Thee.

"JESUS, I COME"

"Resist temptation by making prayer of first importance."

JOHN OWEN

In what ways does our culture make sin seem appealing? What things look sweet but are really destructive? How can God help us when we are being tempted?

⊠ APPLY

This week, identify areas of temptation in your life. Come to the Lord in prayer, confessing your weaknesses and asking for His help. Trust that He will rescue you.

⊠ CONNECT WITH GOD

Heavenly Father, I confess that I am sometimes fooled by sin. It seems so beautiful, and so I draw nearer to sample it—until I feel trapped and see it for the ugly thing it really is. Thank You for rescuing me; thank You that I am no longer trapped in Satan's kingdom. Help me to turn to You each time I feel sin calling me. Teach me the humility to admit my weakness and call for Your rescue.

Keep your servant from deliberate sins!
Don't let them control me.
Then I will be free of guilt
and innocent of great sin.

PSALM 19:13

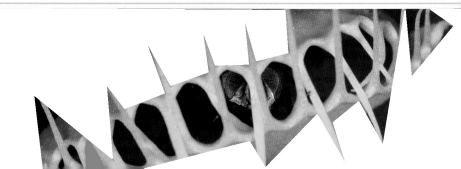

48

Seeking Humility

Dress yourselves in humility as you relate to one another, for

"God opposes the proud
but gives grace to the humble."

1 PETER 5:5

RICK CALLED ME into the dining room one morning. Right out front were three tom turkeys puffed up, tail feathers spread in all their magnificence—and one plain little tina turkey pecking at tidbits in our garden. Faces purple and red, the boys strutted this way and that. One even did a side walking routine that had Rick and me laughing inside the house. Soon another two toms showed up. I guess this was a gorgeous hen.

She paid no attention. Aloof, she focused on the food in front of her slender face. Peck. Peck. Peck-peck-peck. One young tom approached in all his glory, and when she looked at him, you could see him puff up with pride. Three others thought enough was enough and approached him. He deflated like a balloon and shot down the street. Another gave up and wandered off. Miss Hen ignored the three remaining suitors.

We left them to their courtship ritual and got ready for church. As we drove down the road, there they were, the three puffed-up toms, still trying to woo the hen's favors. She was perched on the wood fence looking down her beak at them.

The strutting tom turkeys made us laugh, but pride is never funny or attractive. "Look at me; look at me" is often the cry of a child who wants all the attention fixed on me, me, me! Pride keeps us focused on ourselves and prevents us from turning to God. Relationships suffer and die when we cling to pride, because we're so worried about ourselves that we can't spare any energy to care genuinely for others.

The antidote to pride is humility. God calls us to "dress ourselves"

with humility and promises He will give grace to the humble—to those who understand that He is Lord and they are not.

People can certainly make turkeys out of themselves. King Solomon stated it bluntly in the book of Proverbs: "Pride leads to disgrace, but with humility comes wisdom" (11:2). Tom Turkey might have been more successful if he'd been feathered with humility.

> *Have Thine own way, Lord! Have Thine own way!*
> *Thou art the potter; I am the clay.*
> *Mold me and make me after Thy will,*
> *While I am waiting, yielded and still.*
>
> "HAVE THINE OWN WAY, LORD"

REFLECT

Think back on a time when you reacted to a situation out of pride rather than humility. What was the result? How can pride blind us to the needs of others around us and keep us at arm's length from God?

APPLY

This week, reflect on what triggers you to react with pride. Meditate on Proverbs 11:2 or 1 Peter 5:5 and ask God to help you let go of pride and develop humility.

CONNECT WITH GOD

Dear Lord, so often I react with pride because I feel threatened. I'm worried about being respected or about getting what I think I deserve. It's exhausting to care so much about what others think of me, and I know sometimes I'm just making a fool of myself. Please help me to respond out of humility instead of pride. Teach me to remember that You are God and I am Your child—no more, no less. I don't have to grasp for what I want because I have everything I need in You.

Though the LORD is great, he cares for the humble,
but he keeps his distance from the proud.

PSALM 138:6

hour
fifty-five

49

Pursuing Peace

*[Jesus said,] "I am leaving you with a gift—peace of mind and heart.
And the peace I give is a gift the world cannot give. So don't be troubled
or afraid."*

JOHN 14:27

MOURNING DOVES come to our bird feeder. They sit together in the branches of our oak, watchful of the hawk that once snatched a quail at the feeder. All we saw was a streak and then a pouf of feathers floating down. It is a bird feeder, after all. We don't discriminate. The doves aren't picky about the feed, but they're careful for their own safety. They're looking for food, not for a fight.

The first time the Bible mentions a dove is after the flood. Noah and his family were safe on the ark, watching as the rain stopped and the earth began to dry out. When Noah thought it might be safe to leave the boat, he sent out a raven, and it just kept flying. If it found a place to land, it didn't return to let Noah know where it was. Next, Noah sent out a dove. At first it was unable to find a place to land, but then it returned holding a sprig from an olive tree—an image that later became a widespread symbol for peace. After a time of judgment and destruction, now God was promising a time of peace and redemption.

Jesus told His disciples not to be afraid, because He was leaving them with "peace of mind and heart" (John 14:27). Anyone who has read the book of Acts knows that even after they received this gift, the disciples' lives did not go smoothly or end well, at least from a human perspective. All of them suffered for sharing the gospel, and many were even martyred. Jesus clearly didn't promise them peaceful circumstances. But He did promise them—and us—peace of mind and heart. We don't have to be troubled or afraid because of the simple fact that God is with us, and He is in control. In John 16:33 Jesus told His disciples why they could have peace: "Here on earth you will have many trials and sorrows. But take heart, because I have overcome the world."

Tides of trouble may come and go, floodwaters may rise, but no matter what the circumstances, the peace of God is always available. He has overcome!

Like a river glorious
Is God's perfect peace,
Over all victorious
In its bright increase;
Perfect, yet it floweth
Fuller ev'ry day,
Perfect, yet it groweth
Deeper all the way.

Stayed upon Jehovah,
Hearts are fully blest—
Finding as He promised
Perfect peace and rest.

"LIKE A RIVER GLORIOUS"

"If God be our God . . .
He will give us peace in trouble: when a storm without,
he will make music within. The world can create trouble
in peace, but God can create peace in trouble."

THOMAS WATSON

❧ REFLECT

What comes to mind when you think of peace? How might our culture's definition be different from the biblical definition?

❧ APPLY

When do you most struggle to rest in God's peace? This week, if you're anxious about your circumstances, take a minute to read Jesus' words in John 14:27 and 16:33 and remember the true source of peace.

❧ CONNECT WITH GOD

Dear Lord, when I seek peace through things or circumstances, help me to remember that You are the true source. You can give peace because You have overcome all the troubles I will face in this world. Help me to trust in You and find that genuine peace of mind and heart.

In peace I will lie down and sleep,
for you alone, O LORD, will keep me safe.

PSALM 4:8

50

Godly Diversity

The human body has many parts, but the many parts make up one whole body. So it is with the body of Christ.

1 CORINTHIANS 12:12

I DID A WORD PUZZLE the other day that astounded me. Among the jumble of letters I had to search out names of beetles: bark, blister, carpet, carrion, chafer, checkered, click, Colorado potato, diving, flat grain, fruitworm, ground, Japanese, june, ladybird, leaf, long-horned, powderpost, rove, seed weevils, sexton, soldier, spider, stag, tiger, whirligig. And this is just a short list of the more than 300,000 species of beetles in the world—beetles God created. Each with a purpose!

Have you ever thought about the number of species and subspecies, each unique, each with a job to do? They're a testimony to God's fantastic design, yet we're supposed to believe they each had to evolve over eons of time. God's Word is filled with information. He must have known mankind would try to cut Him out of the equation of how

"No one is useless in this world . . .
who lightens the burden of it for any one else."

CHARLES DICKENS

life on this planet came to be. Why else would He say repeatedly that each plant and animal would procreate "after their kind"? In other words, each beetle listed above was created and remains as it was when God spoke it into being. Even minor changes due to natural selection—like the beaks of Darwin's finches—do not add up to enough mutations to turn one animal into another kind. From the stars in the heavens to the tiniest part of an atom, all creation cries out glory to the Lord.

Like the many beetles in the world, human beings are also varied and unique. No matter our ethnic heritage or economic background, we are all people with unique gifts God has given for unique purposes in His Kingdom. There are teachers, plumbers, doctors, mechanics, garbage collectors and artists, truck drivers and marathon runners, actors and lawyers. God created with infinite variety, each a wonder to behold.

In the body of Christ, these unique purposes come together into a powerful, coherent whole. God has gifted us differently, but all of the gifts work together to glorify God and further His Kingdom. How boring it would be if we were all alike. The body works best when each of us does our job to the best of our ability, celebrating the marvelous diversity of people around us who are also serving in their appointed place and way.

"The Church is so constituted that every member matters, and matters in a very vital sense."

D. MARTYN LLOYD-JONES

REFLECT

Why do you think God created such an amazing variety of plants, animals, and people? What does this tell us about His character? When have you seen believers work together with their different gifts to meet a common goal?

APPLY

This week, reflect on your own strengths and gifts. What are you best at? What kinds of work or service are you drawn to? Consider how they can fit best in the body of Christ. Give thanks this week for all the different ways God has gifted people in the church.

CONNECT WITH GOD

Creator God, thank You for the amazing variety of creatures You have made. From beetles to flowers to people, You have created with lavishness and abundance. Thank You for making each person unique. Help us to appreciate those differences, especially in the body of believers. May I never waste time wishing I had another's gifts, but instead praise You for the opportunity to be part of the body, working together to glorify You.

Let them praise the name of the LORD,
for at his command they were created,

PSALM 148:5, NIV

51

A Firm Foundation

[Jesus said,] "Anyone who listens to my teaching and follows it is wise, like a person who builds a house on solid rock. Though the rain comes in torrents and the floodwaters rise and the winds beat against that house, it won't collapse because it is built on bedrock. But anyone who hears my teaching and doesn't obey it is foolish, like a person who builds a house on sand. When the rains and floods come and the winds beat against that house, it will collapse with a mighty crash."
MATTHEW 7:24-27

I TOOK THREE of our grandchildren to Doran Beach near Bodega Bay and led them onto the white sand. We carried our buckets, hand rakes and trowels, energy bars and Gatorade until we found the perfect spot: warm sand a hundred feet from the wet sand and ocean waves. I relaxed and watched the children run. One brought back treasures of shells, driftwood, and other flotsam. Naturally, they were tempted by the sand-lapping waves. The Pacific is cold, and they screeched like seagulls when their toes first touched the salt water. Soon they were ankle-deep, then knee-deep.

A few minutes later, one grandchild ended up knocked over by an incoming wave. Another grandchild came to the rescue before I could get there. We were all in the shallows, but sand has a way of getting into your clothing. The fallen child rinsed off in the surf, we rolled up the pant legs, and she was back to exploring.

Sand and waves are a dangerous combination.

When you stand on sand and the waves go out, you can feel the ground beneath your feet being pulled away. If you stand long enough, you get stuck; the waves keep pounding and you sink further in the wet sand that grips your legs. Or you could be knocked over and swept out to sea, maybe carried away by the current or pulled beneath the surface by an undertow. When you're standing on shifting sand instead of solid ground, it's easy to lose your footing.

Jesus' brief parable in Matthew 7 vividly shows the difference between those who base their lives on His teaching and those who ignore it. People who don't heed His words will see their houses (lives) collapse "with a mighty crash" (v. 27) at the first sign of a storm. Only those who have Him for their foundation will stand firm when trouble comes.

I don't want to stand on the ever-shifting sands of the world's philosophies and man-made religions. I want to stand on the solid teachings and promises of God through Christ Jesus who lived, died, arose, and is coming again.

> *My hope is built on nothing less*
> *Than Jesus' blood and righteousness;*
> *I dare not trust the sweetest frame,*
> *But wholly lean on Jesus' name.*
> *On Christ, the solid rock, I stand;*
> *All other ground is sinking sand.*

"THE SOLID ROCK"

[God says,] "When the earth quakes and its people live in turmoil, I am the one who keeps its foundations firm."

PSALM 75:3

✠ REFLECT

What are some things our culture relies on that are really shifting sand? How can we develop a stronger foundation in Christ?

✠ APPLY

This week, spend time pondering Jesus' words about the foolish man and the wise man in Matthew 7. Meditate on some Scripture passages that talk about finding a strong foundation in God: Proverbs 10:25; Isaiah 33:5-6; 1 Peter 5:10.

✠ CONNECT WITH GOD

Lord God, You alone are my firm foundation. I don't want to experience the insecurity that comes from trusting in ideas or people that are constantly changing. Teach me to place my trust in You. Then I know I will not be shaken, no matter what storms come my way.

---

*[God says,] "When the earth quakes and its people live in turmoil,
I am the one who keeps its foundations firm."*

PSALM 75:3

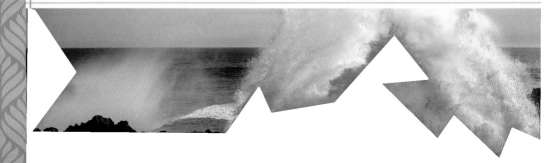

52

Believing in the Unseen

We don't look at the troubles we can see now; rather, we fix our gaze on things that cannot be seen. For the things we see now will soon be gone, but the things we cannot see will last forever.

2 CORINTHIANS 4:18

WHEN RICK AND I were in Alaska a few Septembers ago, we witnessed the most amazing blast of autumn colors coming in. Overnight, the scenery changed from thousands of shades of green to a land carpeted in red and orange, with pops of gold and yellow. We stood on our hotel balcony and drank it all in.

What's amazing is that the autumn colors are always there, even when we can't see them. During spring and summer, leaves produce the chlorophyll responsible for their green color. Chlorophyll is the compound that harnesses energy from sunlight, triggering the photosynthesis process that converts water and carbon dioxide into food. The shortened days of autumn bring colder temperatures and fewer hours of sunlight, meaning less chlorophyll is produced. Without chlorophyll to make the leaves green, other pigments—which have

been present all along—reveal the reds, oranges, yellows, and golds that have been hidden during the light-bright days.

How like God—always there even when we can't see Him. Jesus' twelve disciples were among the few people through all of history fortunate enough to see God in the flesh, to walk so closely with Him that they could never doubt His existence. But those of us who live in this time after Jesus' ascension must worship a God we cannot see. We must have faith that God is present even when we can't tell that He is there, even when the sin and selfishness of this world blind us to the deeper reality of the spiritual realm.

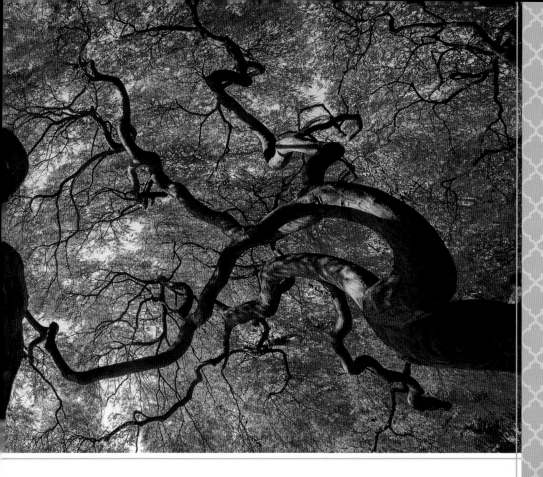

Sometimes it's hard to believe in something so intangible. Yet the apostle Paul reminds us of the paradoxical truth: what is invisible is more real and more permanent than what is visible. The things we can see and touch right now will "soon be gone," as 2 Corinthians 4:18 says, but the unseen—our faith, heaven, God Himself—will last forever.

"I believe in Christianity as I believe that the Sun has risen, not only because I see it, but because by it I see everything else."

C. S. LEWIS

REFLECT

Why can it be so difficult to believe in something we cannot see? How should we handle our doubts? How can the Bible and other testimonies of faith strengthen our trust in God's presence?

APPLY

This week, take a minute each day to remember that this life is not the greatest reality. God is. Let that seep into your thoughts and bring you comfort and renewed purpose.

CONNECT WITH GOD

Heavenly Father, I confess that I sometimes struggle to believe in what I cannot see. Yet I know You are there, because I have experienced Your work in the world and I have read Your life-giving Word. Help me to remember that You *are the greatest reality, not the tensions of my day-to-day life. May I always fix my eyes on You.*

Your unfailing love will last forever.
Your faithfulness is as enduring as the heavens.

PSALM 89:2

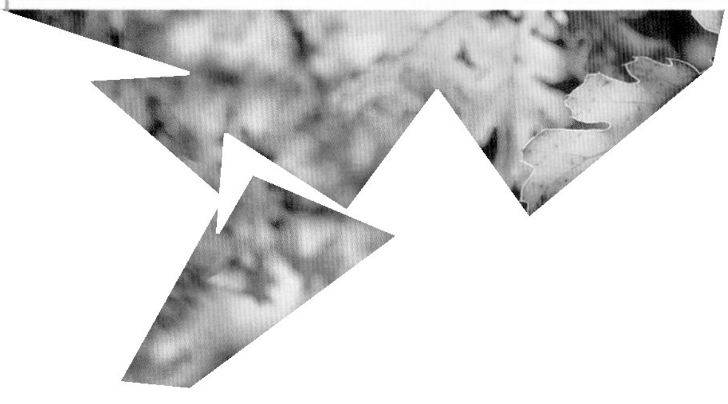

About the Authors

New York Times bestselling author FRANCINE RIVERS had a successful writing career in the general market for several years before becoming a born-again Christian. As her statement of faith, she wrote *Redeeming Love,* a retelling of the biblical story of Gomer and Hosea set during the time of the California Gold Rush. *Redeeming Love* is now considered by many to be a classic work of Christian fiction, and it continues to be one of the industry's top-selling titles year after year.

Since *Redeeming Love,* Francine has published numerous novels with Christian themes—all bestsellers—and she has continued to win both industry acclaim and reader loyalty around the world. Her Christian novels have been awarded or nominated for many honors, and in 1997, after winning her third RITA Award for inspirational fiction, Francine was inducted into the Romance Writers of America's Hall of Fame. In 2015, she received the Lifetime Achievement Award from American Christian Fiction Writers (ACFW).

Francine's novels have been translated into over thirty different languages, and she enjoys bestseller status in many foreign countries.

Francine and her husband live in northern California and enjoy time spent with their grown children and grandchildren. She uses her writing to draw closer to the Lord, and she desires that through her work she might worship and praise Jesus for all He has done and is doing in her life.

Visit her website at www.francinerivers.com and connect with her on Facebook (www.facebook.com/FrancineRivers) and Twitter (@FrancineRivers).

KARIN STOCK BUURSMA has worked in publishing for more than fifteen years, first at a publishing house and now as a freelance editor and writer. She lives in Wheaton, Illinois, with her husband and two daughters.

IMAGE CREDITS

Damask pattern © Debra Hughes/ Shutterstock

Vintage pattern © Watchada/Dollar Photo Club

Quatrefoil pattern © relich/Dollar Photo Club

Adorn font © Laura Worthington/Creative Market

Contents Pulpit rock © Zak Suhar/Snapwi.re

Epigraph Sunburst © TSV Creative/Creative Market

Introduction Plants by Annie Spratt/Unsplash .com

Chapter 1 Sunrise in grass by Rose Erkul/ Unsplash.com. Sunrise by Shane Perry/ Unsplash.com.

Chapter 2 Woodpecker © Marcel/Stocksy. Great spotted woodpecker © cat_smile/ Dollar Photo Club.

Chapter 3 Apple tree © Voyagerix/Dollar Photo Club

Chapter 4 Bobwhite quails © Jeremy Woodhouse/Blend Images/Corbis. Male quail © Denalli/500px.

Chapter 5 Desert © 145/John Wang/Ocean/ Corbis. Dandelion by Paul Talbot/ Unsplash.com.

Chapter 6 Ant rescue © Iwan Ramawan/500px. Ant by David Higgins/Unsplash.com.

Chapter 7 Sequoia and forest path © Galyna Andrushko/Dollar Photo Club

Chapter 8 Beetle © Martin Harvey/Corbis. Desert by Tim de Groot/Unsplash.com. Fawn © Erik de Klerck/500px.

Chapter 9 Misty path © liv4u/Dollar Photo Club

Chapter 10 Seagull by Nichole Thrasher/ Unsplash.com. Seagull flying by Rod Long/Unsplash.com.

Chapter 11 Lilac © abidika/Dollar Photo Club. Snow-covered branch © avtk/Dollar Photo Club.

Chapter 12 Squirrel and lupine © Geert Weggen/500px. Squirrel and bird © Andre Villeneuve/500px.

Chapter 13 Sweet peas © Georgianna Lane/ Garden Photo World/Corbis. Sweet pea © Photozi/Dollar Photo Club.

Chapter 14 Mouse © Geert Weggen/500px. Sarge © Elaina Burdo.

Chapter 15 Window © catalinbalau/Dollar Photo Club. Geranium © UlrikeAdam/ Dollar Photo Club.

Chapter 16 Hiding turtle © backyardphoto/ Dollar Photo Club. Turtle © panjapone/ Dollar Photo Club.

Chapter 17 Pansies © Thomas Jäger/ Westend61/Corbis. Pansy in concrete © karkairane/Dollar Photo Club.

Chapter 18 Eagle © wojciech nowak/Dollar Photo Club. Hawk by Jeremy Cai/Unsplash .com.

Chapter 19 Glacier by Guillermo Riquelme/ Unsplash.com